WELCOME!

On behalf of Splash! Publications, we would like to welcome you to *New World Explorers*, one of several books in our American History series. Since this curriculum was designed by teachers, we are positive that you will find it to be the most comprehensive program you have ever utilized to teach students about explorers of the New World. We would like to take a few moments to familiarize you with the program.

THE FORMAT

New World Explorers is a nine lesson program. Our goal is a curriculum that you can use the very first day you purchase our materials. No lessons to plan, comprehension questions to write, activities to create, or vocabulary words to define. Simply open the book and start teaching.

Each of the nine lessons requires students to complete vocabulary cards, read about one of the New World explorers, and complete a comprehension activity that will expose them to various standardized test formats. In addition, each lesson includes a balanced mix of lower and higher level activities for students to complete. Vocabulary quizzes, cardinal direction and scale mapping activities, research projects utilizing primary and secondary sources and graphic organizers, writing activities, time lines, and following written directions are the types of activities that will guide students through their journey of *New World Explorers*.

THE LESSON PLANS

On the next several pages, you will find the Lesson Plans for *New World Explorers*. The Lesson Plans clearly outline what students must do before, during, and after each lesson. Page numbers are listed so that you will immediately know what you need to photocopy before beginning each lesson. The answers to all activities, quizzes, and comprehension questions are located on pages 82-86.

NOTE: Students will complete a culminating activity at the end of the unit. We suggest that students keep the information from each lesson in a notebook or folder.

THE VOCABULARY

Each lesson features words in bold type. We have included a Glossary on pages 77-81 to help students pronounce and define the words. Unlike a dictionary, the definitions in the Glossary are concise and written in context. Remember, we're teachers! Students will be exposed to these vocabulary words in the comprehension activities. They will also be tested on the vocabulary words four times throughout their study of *New World Explorers*.

Students will be responsible for filling out and studying the vocabulary cards. You may want to have students bring in a small box for storing their vocabulary cards. We don't have to tell you that incorporating these words into your Reading and Spelling programs will save time and make the words more meaningful for students.

Core Standards: The "Big Ideas"

Core Standards help teachers prioritize instruction and connect the "big ideas" students need to know in order to advance. As a reading-based unit, *New World Explorers* fosters literacy in Social Studies.

At the same time that students are learning important factual content about *New World Explorers*, they are meeting the Common Core Standards for English Language Arts and making connections to the "big ideas" in American History. Alignment to the 3rd-5th Grade Common Core Standards is clearly noted in the Lesson Plans. Below is the legend used to abbreviate the Common Core Strands:

Common Core Strand Code:
CC = Common Core
RL = Reading-Literature
RI = Reading Informational Text
RF = Reading Foundations Skills
W = Writing
SL = Speaking Listening
L = Language

The Copyright

Our Other Titles

Complete State History Programs

Do American History!
Do Arizona!
Do California!
Do Colorado!
Do Florida!
Do Nevada!
Do New Mexico!
Do Texas!
Do Washington!

Literature Study Guides

Charlotte's Web
Cricket in Times Square
Enormous Egg
Sarah, Plain and Tall

Primary Series

Leveled Math: Addition Bk 1
Leveled Math: Addition Bk 2
Leveled Math: Subtraction Bk 1
Leveled Math: Subtraction Bk 2
National Holidays
National Symbols
Poems for Every Holiday
Poems for Every Season

American History Series

Spanish Explorers & Conquistadors
The Thirteen Original Colonies
Early American Government
The American Revolution
Slavery in America
The Civil War
Westward Expansion

U.S. Region Series

The Middle Atlantic States
The New England States
The Great Lakes States
The Great Plains States
The Southeast States
The Southwest States
The Mountain States
The Pacific States

State History Series

Arizona Geography
Arizona Animals
Arizona History
Arizona Government & Economy
California Geography
California Animals
California History
California Government & Economy
Florida Geography
Florida Animals
Florida History
Florida Government & Economy
Illinois History
Indiana History
Michigan History
Ohio History
Texas Geography
Texas Animals
Texas History
Texas Government & Economy

TABLE OF CONTENTS

NEW WORLD EXPLORERS

TABLE OF CONTENTS

NEW WORLD EXPLORERS (CONTINUED)

LESSONS *at a* GLANCE

1. Before reading Leif Erikson, students will:
- complete Vocabulary Cards for *accused, A.D., archaeologists, artifacts, barren, bay, climate, coast, colonists, convinced, Europe, foreign, founded, glaciers, harbor, herds, historians, island, livestock, longhouses, meadows, Newfoundland, New World, Norway, Viking, voyage.* *(pg. 1)*

After reading Leif Erikson *(pps. 2-3)*, students will:
- answer Leif Erikson Reading Comprehension Questions. *(pg. 4)*
- follow written directions to make a miniature Viking ship. *(pps. 5-14)*
- take a Vocabulary Quiz for New World Explorers Part I. *(pps. 15-16)*

THE LEIF ERIKSON LESSON IS ALIGNED WITH THESE 3RD-5TH GRADE CORE STANDARDS:
CC.RI.1, CC.RI.2, CC.RI.3, CC.RI.4, CC.RI.7, CC.RI.10, CC.RF.3A, CC.RF.4A, CC.RF.4C, CC.L.4A, CC.L.4C, CC.L.6

2. Before reading John Cabot, students will:
- complete Vocabulary Cards for *admiral, Asia, astronomy, autobiography, biographies, conflicts, departed, expedition, investigate, mariner, merchant, monopoly, navigators, North America, ports, Portugal, profits, promoted, West Indies.* *(pg. 1)*

After reading John Cabot *(pps. 17-19)*, students will:
- answer John Cabot Reading Comprehension Questions. *(pg. 20)*
- differentiate between primary and secondary sources. *(pg. 21)*

THE JOHN CABOT LESSON IS ALIGNED WITH THESE 3RD-5TH GRADE CORE STANDARDS:
CC.RI.1, CC.RI.2, CC.RI.3, CC.RI.4, CC.RI.6, CC.RI.7, CC.RI.10, CC.RF.3A, CC.RF.4A, CC.RF.4C, CC.L.4A, CC.L.4C, CC.L.6

LESSONS at a GLANCE

3. Before reading Giovanni da Verrazano, students will:
- complete Vocabulary Cards for *anchored, cannibals, Caribbean, century, conquistadors, journals, natives, raiding, sound.* *(pg. 1)*

After reading Giovanni da Verrazano *(pps. 22-23)*, students will:
- answer Giovanni da Verrazano Questions. *(pg. 24)*
- take a Vocabulary Quiz for New World Explorers Part II. *(pps. 25-26)*

THE GIOVANNI DA VERRAZANO LESSON IS ALIGNED WITH THESE 3RD-5TH GRADE CORE STANDARDS: CC.RI.1, CC.RI.2, CC.RI.3, CC.RI.4, CC.RI.7, CC.RI.10, CC.RF.3A, CC.RF.4A, CC.RF.4C, CC.L.4A, CC.L.4C, CC.L.6

4. Before reading Jacques Cartier, students will:
- complete Vocabulary Cards for *abandoned, harsh, hostile, kidnapped, loincloths, New France, peninsula, Québec, reunited, scurvy.* *(pg. 1)*

After reading Jacques Cartier *(pps. 27-29)*, students will:
- answer Jacques Cartier Reading Comprehension Questions. *(pg. 30)*
- create a time line for Jacques Cartier in Time Travel Part I. *(pg. 31)*
- create a personal time line in Time Travel Part II. *(pg. 32)*

THE JACQUES CARTIER LESSON IS ALIGNED WITH THESE 3RD-5TH GRADE CORE STANDARDS: CC.RI.1, CC.RI.2, CC.RI.3, CC.RI.4, CC.RI.6, CC.RI.7, CC.RI.10, CC.RF.3A, CC.RF.4A, CC.RF.4C, CC.L.4A, CC.L.4C, CC.L.6

LESSONS at a GLANCE

5. Before reading Sir Francis Drake, students will:
- complete Vocabulary Cards for *appointed, Armada, aviary, beheaded, bluffs, buttes, cargo, channel, defeating, elevations, endangered, English Channel, exhibits, extends, fleet, formations, habitats, immigrants, invading, knight, petroglyphs, plundered, preserve, privateer, revenge, Strait of Magellan, vessel, western hemisphere. (pg. 1)*

After reading Sir Francis Drake *(pps. 33-35)*, students will:
- answer Sir Francis Drake Reading Comprehension Questions. *(pg. 36)*
- use cardinal and intermediate directions to plot California points of interest on a map. *(pps. 37-41)*
- take a Vocabulary Quiz for New World Explorers Part III. *(pps. 42-43)*

THE SIR FRANCIS DRAKE LESSON IS ALIGNED WITH THESE 3RD-5TH GRADE CORE STANDARDS: CC.RI.1, CC.RI.2, CC.RI.3, CC.RI.4, CC.RI.7, CC.RI.10, CC.RF.3A, CC.RF.4A, CC.RF.4C, CC.L.4A, CC.L.4C, CC.L.6

6. Before reading Samuel de Champlain, students will:
- complete Vocabulary Cards for *allies, conquering, flee, geographer, military, moat, musket, resources, smallpox, stroke, treaties. (pg. 1)*

After reading Samuel de Champlain *(pps. 44-47)*, students will:
- answer Samuel de Champlain Reading Comprehension Questions. *(pg. 48)*
- plot islands, water resources, and Champlain's voyages on a map. *(pps. 49-50)*

THE SAMUEL DE CHAMPLAIN LESSON IS ALIGNED WITH THESE 3RD-5TH GRADE CORE STANDARDS: CC.RI.1, CC.RI.2, CC.RI.3, CC.RI.4, CC.RI.7, CC.RI.10, CC.RF.3A, CC.RF.4A, CC.RF.4C, CC.L.4A, CC.L.4C, CC.L.6

LESSONS *at a* GLANCE

7. Before reading Henry Hudson, students will:
- complete Vocabulary Cards for *Amsterdam, captives, errands, industry, kilometers, North Pole, pods, rival, treason.* *(pg. 1)*

After reading Henry Hudson *(pps. 51-54)*, students will:
- answer Henry Hudson Reading Comprehension Questions. *(pg. 55)*
- use scale rulers to measure the distance of each of Hudson's four voyages. *(pps. 56-61)*

THE HENRY HUDSON LESSON IS ALIGNED WITH THESE 3RD-5TH GRADE CORE STANDARDS:
CC.RI.1, CC.RI.2, CC.RI.3, CC.RI.4, CC.RI.7, CC.RI.10, CC.RF.3A, CC.RF.4A, CC.RF.4C, CC.L.4A, CC.L.4C, CC.L.6

8. Before reading Robert La Salle, students will:
- complete Vocabulary Cards for *governor, Great Lakes, Jesuit, missionary, missions, nobility, vows, whirlpools.* *(pg. 1)*

After reading Robert La Salle *(pps. 62-66)*, students will:
- answer Robert La Salle Reading Comprehension Questions. *(pg. 67)*
- research a famous explorer to complete K•W•L•H chart. *(pps. 68-70)*
- use K•W•L•H chart to answer famous explorer discussion questions. *(pg. 71)*

THE ROBERT LA SALLE LESSON IS ALIGNED WITH THESE 3RD-5TH GRADE CORE STANDARDS:
CC.RI.1, CC.RI.2, CC.RI.3, CC.RI.4, CC.RI.6, CC.RI.7, CC.RI.10, CC.RF.3A, CC.RF.4A, CC.RF.4C, CC.W.1A, CC.W.1B, CC.W.7, CC.W.8, CC.W.9B, CC.L.4A, CC.L.4C, CC.L.6

9. Before reading The Future of New France, students will:
- complete Vocabulary Cards for *fertile, Great Britain, militias, outnumbered, scalped, surrendered.* *(pg. 1)*

After reading The Future of New France *(pps. 72-73)*, students will:
- answer The Future of New France Reading Comprehension Questions. *(pg. 74)*
- take a Vocabulary Quiz for New World Explorers Part IV. *(pps. 75-76)*

THE FUTURE OF NEW FRANCE LESSON IS ALIGNED WITH THESE 3RD-5TH GRADE CORE STANDARDS:
CC.RI.1, CC.RI.2, CC.RI.3, CC.RI.4, CC.RI.6, CC.RI.7, CC.RI.10, CC.RF.3A, CC.RF.4A, CC.RF.4C, CC.L.4A, CC.L.4C, CC.L.6

VOCABULARY CARD

word: _____

definition: _____

_____

VOCABULARY CARD

word: _____

definition: _____

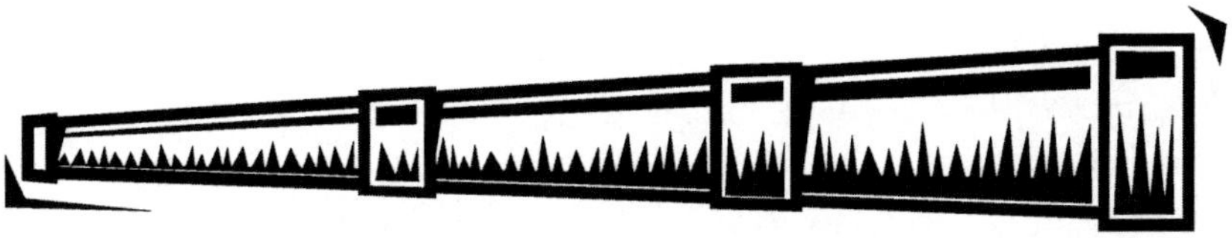

_____

VOCABULARY CARD

word: _____

definition: _____

_____

Leif Erikson

Leif Erikson was born in Iceland. **Historians** are not sure exactly when he was born, but most agree that it was around 970 **A.D.** Leif was the son of famous **Viking** explorer Erik the Red. The Vikings were the best ship builders in **Europe.** They used their ships to explore the rough waters of the Northern Atlantic Ocean.

Leif's Early Years

Like other Viking children, Leif did not spend his early years with his family. At eight years old, Leif was sent to **Norway** where he learned to read, write, solve problems, and speak **foreign** languages. He was also taught how to farm and use weapons. During his free time, Leif watched the ships come into the **harbor**.

At the age of 12, Leif was considered a man. He moved back to his family's farm. In the four years since he had been gone, the farm had grown to include several houses, **herds** of animals, and slaves.

Discovering Greenland

In 982, Erik the Red was **accused** of murder and forced to leave Iceland for three years. He sailed west with his wife, four children, and a few slaves. The family spent the next three years exploring an **island** that Erik the Red named Greenland.

In 985, Erik the Red returned to Iceland. He told about his adventures and **convinced** a large group of people to return to Greenland with him.

In the spring of 985, Erik loaded 25 ships with supplies, settlers, and **livestock**. The **voyage** was a disaster. The waves were too strong for the ships. Many were forced to turn back. Others disappeared and were never seen again. Only 350 **colonists** and 14 ships actually made it to Greenland. The survivors **founded** two colonies on the southwest **coast** of Greenland. The

Leif Erikson

colonists found the land in this area of Greenland perfect for farming. When the weather was warm, groups of men traveled to Disko **Bay** to hunt for seals and beached whales.

LEIF ERIKSON'S VOYAGE TO THE NEW WORLD

In 1003, Leif Erikson bought his first boat. He hired a crew of 35 men and set out on a voyage. They sailed west of Greenland and discovered **barren** land that was covered with **glaciers** (GLAY•shers) and flat, shiny rocks. Leif named the area Helluland, which means "land of the flat stones." Historians believe that Helluland is Baffin Island, the largest island in present-day Canada.

Continuing south, Leif and his crew discovered a flat piece of land that was covered with trees and white sandy beaches. Leif named this area Markland, which means "land covered with wood." Historians agree that Markland is present-day Labrador on the east coast of Canada.

Southeast of Markland, Leif Erikson came upon an island that was covered with grassy **meadows** and grape vines. He named the island Vinland which means "wine land."

There were plenty of salmon in Vinland's rivers and the **climate** was mild. They built a small settlement and stayed in Vinland during the winter. A year later, Leif's father Erik died. Leif returned to Greenland and took control of his family's farm.

PROOF OF ERIKSON'S DISCOVERIES

In 1960, **archaeologists** (ar•kee•OL•uh•jists) Helge Ingstad and his wife Ann Stine Ingstad traveled to the northern tip of **Newfoundland** where they believe Vinland was located. The Ingstads found the remains of Viking **longhouses** that were 72 feet long and 50 feet wide. The archaeologists also uncovered **artifacts** that included tools for weaving, carving wood, bending iron, and building boats. If the archaeologists' discoveries are true, Leif Erikson discovered the **New World** almost 500 years before famous explorer Christopher Columbus.

≋≋≋≋≋ LEIF ERIKSON ≋≋≋≋≋

Directions: Read each question carefully. Darken the circle for the correct answer.

1. **After reading the first paragraph about Leif Erikson, you learn that –**

   A historians aren't sure where he was born

   B he was the son a famous Spanish explorer

   C his father was Erik the Red

   D the Vikings explored the Pacific Ocean

2. **Which part about Leif Erikson's early life might seem strange to <u>most</u> people?**

   F He learned to read and write.

   G He learned foreign languages.

   H He watched ships come into the harbor during his free time.

   J He did not spend part of his childhood with his family.

3. **Why did Leif Erikson's family leave Iceland in 982?**

   A His father had been accused of a crime.

   B Leif's family wanted to explore other islands.

   C Leif's sister was sick and the family needed to find a cure for her illness.

   D Erik the Red wanted to visit his parents in Greenland.

4. **Which phrase tells you that Erik the Red's voyage to build a colony in Greenland was a disaster?**

   F ...loaded 25 ships with supplies...

   G ...founded two colonies on the southwest coast of Greenland...

   H ...only 350 colonists and 14 ships actually made it to Greenland...

   J ...found the land in this area of Greenland perfect for farming...

5. **If Leif Erikson was born in 970 A.D., how old was he when he bought his first boat?**

   A 33

   B 43

   C 67

   D 22

6. **What can you learn from studying the map of Leif Erikson's voyage to the New World?**

   F His voyage started in Iceland.

   G After reaching Helluland, his voyage headed north.

   H The voyage sailed through the Greenland Sea.

   J After reaching Markland, the voyage continued south.

7. **According to the map, Vinland was located –**

   A north of Greenland

   B east of Iceland

   C in Baffin Bay

   D south of Disko Bay

8. **If archaeologists' discoveries are true, who discovered the New World <u>first</u>?**

   F Erik the Red

   G Leif Erikson

   H Christopher Columbus

   J Ann Stine Ingstad

Answers   **READING**

1	Ⓐ Ⓑ Ⓒ Ⓓ	5	Ⓐ Ⓑ Ⓒ Ⓓ
2	Ⓕ Ⓖ Ⓗ Ⓙ	6	Ⓕ Ⓖ Ⓗ Ⓙ
3	Ⓐ Ⓑ Ⓒ Ⓓ	7	Ⓐ Ⓑ Ⓒ Ⓓ
4	Ⓕ Ⓖ Ⓗ Ⓙ	8	Ⓕ Ⓖ Ⓗ Ⓙ

The Vikings were once the best ship builders in Europe. Their ships were sturdy enough to sail the rough waters of the Northern Atlantic Ocean.

In this activity, you will follow written directions to make a miniature Viking ship like the one Leif Erikson used to discover the New World.

1. Color the Inside Ship Pattern brown.

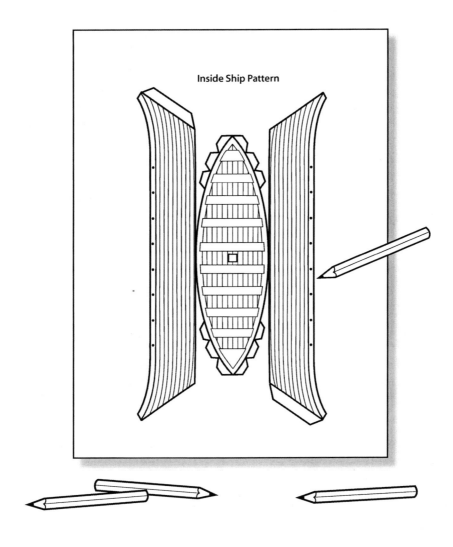

Inside Ship Pattern

2. Use your scissors to carefully cut out the Inside Ship Pattern. As shown below, fold up all tabs on ship's bottom. Glue tabs to the outer side of the ship where the paper is blank.

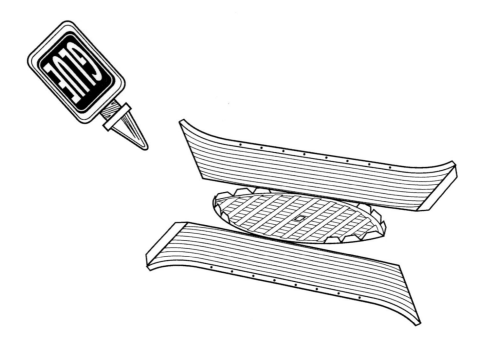

3. Fold the tabs over and glue the ship's sides together as shown. Again, notice that you are gluing the tabs to the outer sides of the ship where the paper is blank.

4. Color the Outside Ship Pattern. The circles are the Viking's shields and should be colored blue, red, orange, yellow, and green.

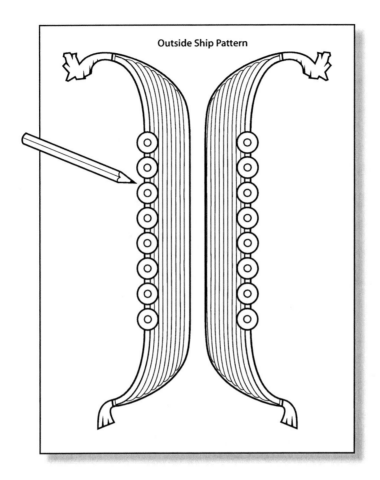

5. Use your scissors to cut out the Outside Ship Pattern.

Glue the Dragon Heads of the pattern together first. Only glue to the line marked by the arrow.

Then glue the Outside Ship Pattern together as shown.

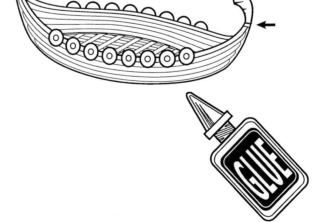

6. Color the Mast and the Top Beam brown. Color the Sail with red and white stripes.

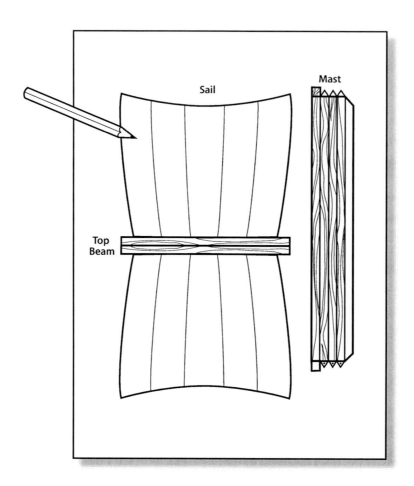

7. Use your scissors to cut out the Sail.

Fold the Sail in half and glue the two sides together as shown.

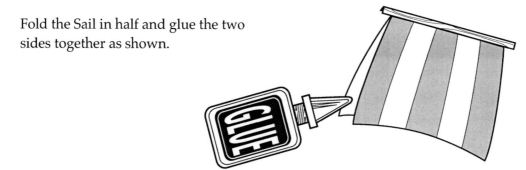

8. Use your scissors to cut out the Mast. Fold on the lines as shown.

9. Glue the Tab under. Let the glue dry before moving on to Step 10.

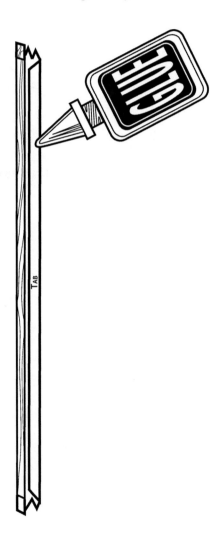

10. Fold triangle tabs down on both the top and the bottom of the Mast.

11. Fold and glue the squares to top and bottom of Mast.

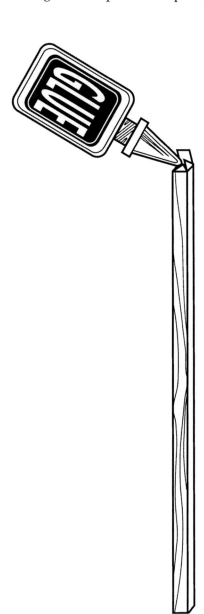

12. Glue the Sail to the Mast. (To make it look real, bend the Sail so it looks like its blowing in the wind.)

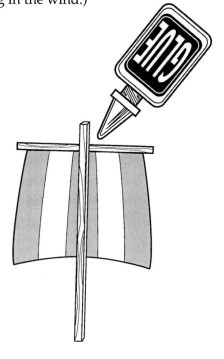

13. Glue bottom square on Mast to square on the bottom of the Ship.

14. Set your finished Ship aside to dry.

Inside Ship Pattern

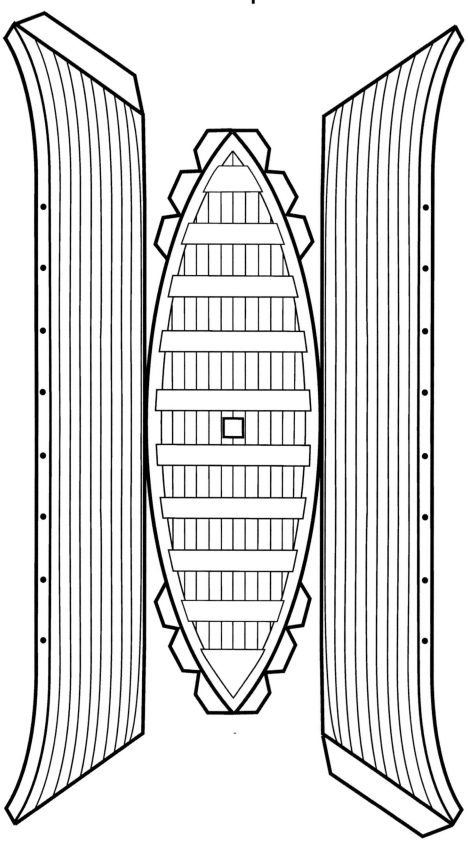

Outside Ship Pattern

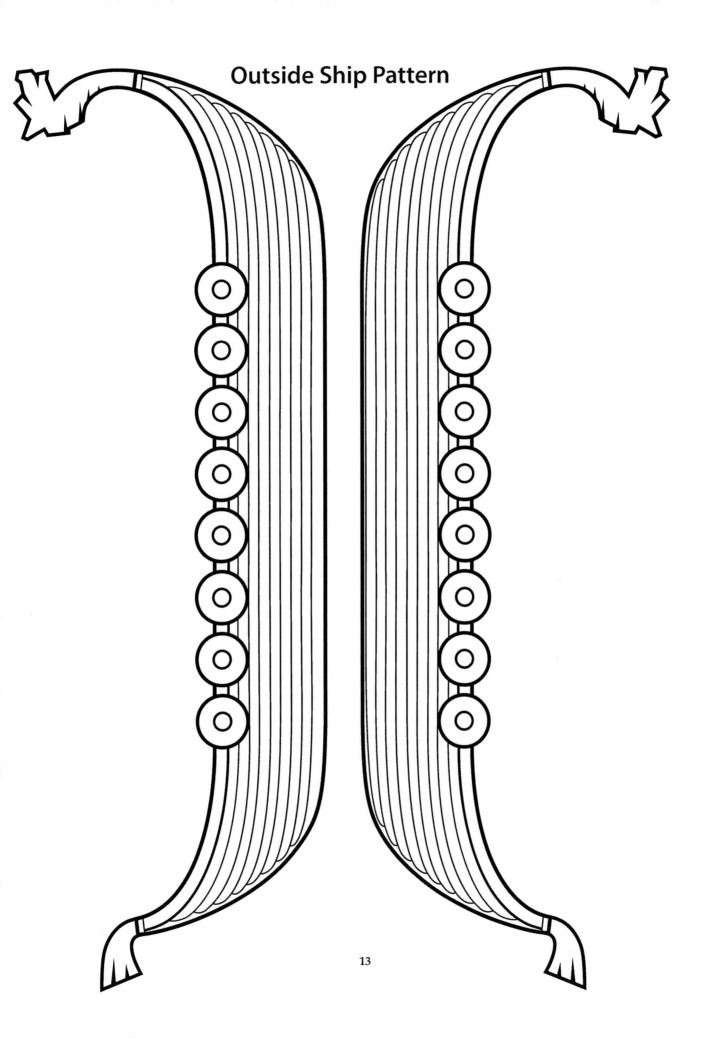

Sail

Mast

≋ VOCABULARY QUIZ ≋

NEW WORLD EXPLORERS
PART I

Directions: Match the vocabulary word on the left with its definition on the right. Put the letter for the definition on the blank next to the vocabulary word it matches. Use each word and definition only once.

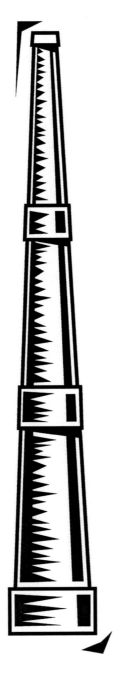

1. _____ accused

2. _____ voyage

3. _____ Viking

4. _____ A.D.

5. _____ archaeologists

6. _____ Norway

7. _____ artifacts

8. _____ barren

9. _____ New World

10. _____ founded

11. _____ historians

12. _____ island

13. _____ livestock

14. _____ bay

15. _____ climate

16. _____ longhouses

A. a European country located in western Scandinavia whose capital and largest city is Oslo.

B. the average weather conditions of an area over a period of years.

C. a journey that is usually made by water.

D. people who are ruled by another country.

E. the period in history after the birth of Jesus Christ.

F. large bodies of ice moving slowly down a valley or spreading across the surface of the land.

G. large areas of grassland.

H. blamed or charged with a crime.

I. people who study history.

J. talked someone into doing something your way.

K. area of land that is completely surrounded by water.

L. started or established.

M. an area of land that borders water.

17. _____ meadows

18. _____ coast

19. _____ Newfoundland

20. _____ herds

21. _____ colonists

22. _____ historians

23. _____ glaciers

24. _____ convinced

25. _____ Europe

26. _____ foreign

N. empty; unable to produce any crops.

O. animals raised on a farm to eat or sell for profit.

P. objects and tools used by early humans for eating, cooking, and hunting.

Q. long dwellings where many families live at the same time.

R. scientists who study past human life by looking at prehistoric fossils and tools.

S. a term once used to describe the continents of North America and South America.

T. people who study history.

U. a body of water surrounded by land that opens to the sea.

V. groups of animals.

W. a sea pirate from Scandinavia.

X. from another country or nation.

Y. the sixth smallest of Earth's seven continents.

Z. a large island in east Canada.

JOHN CABOT

John Cabot was born in Genoa, Italy. Historians aren't sure exactly when John Cabot was born, but most agree that it was around 1455. He was the son of an Italian **merchant**. When John was 11 years old, his family moved to the Italian city of Venice.

Like his father and many other Italians, John became a merchant. He traded valuable Asian spices, silks, stones, and metals throughout the **ports** of the eastern Mediterranean Ocean. These items were bought from traders in **Asia** and sold for very high **profits** in Europe.

During his travels, John became an expert **mariner**. In 1490, John Cabot moved to Spain. Like other explorers and **navigators** you will read about, Cabot wanted to become famous exploring the Atlantic Ocean and finding a safe water route to Asia and its riches.

FINDING A ROUTE TO ASIA

Finding a water route to Asia was very important to leaders in England, France, **Portugal** (POR•chuw•gal), and Spain. In Asia, they could buy jewels, silk, and spices not available in Europe. Italian traders had a **monopoly** on trade with Asia. The Italian traders purchased the items in Asia and sold them at very high prices to Europeans. If England, France, Portugal, and Spain found a safe water route to Asia, they could take control of the Asian trade and buy the things they wanted without paying the Italian traders anything.

JOHN CABOT

FAST FACTS

- The Italian word Caboto means "coastal seaman" in English. Caboto was a common name given to sailors and **navigators**.
- Mapmaking was an important skill taught in Italy. Growing up in Venice gave John an excellent education in mapmaking, navigation, **astronomy**, and mathematics.
- In 1474, John Cabot married a girl named Mattea. The Cabots had three sons. His son Sebastian grew up to be a mapmaker and navigator just like his father.

OTHER ROUTES TO ASIA

Portuguese explorers searched for an eastward route to Asia. They started in Europe and sailed around the tip of Africa. Violent storms in this part of the Atlantic Ocean made this route very dangerous.

In 1492, Spanish explorer Christopher Columbus sailed west to search for a safer route to Asia. Instead of sailing to Asia, Columbus landed off the coast of **North America** in the **West Indies**. He convinced leaders in Spain that he had actually been to Asia.

Portugal and Spain believed that they had found the best water route to Asia. John Cabot was certain that he could find a quicker and safer route to Asia. Neither country was interested in supporting a voyage by John Cabot.

- - - - CHRISTOPHER COLUMBUS
——— PORTUGUESE EXPLORERS

JOHN CABOT'S FIRST VOYAGE

In 1495, John Cabot traveled to England. He told King Henry VII of his plan to reach Asia by sailing west across the Northern Atlantic Ocean. A group of English merchants agreed to support Cabot's plan. King Henry VII gave Cabot and his sons permission to sail to all parts "of the eastern, western, and northern sea to discover and **investigate**." Of course, all new land that Cabot might discover would be claimed by England.

In 1496, John Cabot sailed from England with one ship. The **expedition** was a complete failure. He sailed as far as Iceland, but his ship ran into bad weather. There were constant **conflicts** between Cabot and his crew. To make matters worse, the group ran out of food. Cabot was forced to sail back to England.

CABOT'S SECOND VOYAGE

A year later, Cabot was ready to try again. In May 1497, Cabot left England with one ship and 18 crew members. They sailed west to Dursey Head, Ireland. From Ireland they continued west until they landed on the coast of Newfoundland. Some historians believe that the ship may have actually landed in Nova Scotia, Labrador, or even Maine in the present-day United States. John Cabot thought he had reached Asia. He went ashore, claimed the land for England, and spent some time exploring. In July, Cabot and his crew sailed home to England.

John Cabot received a hero's welcome in England. Everyone thought he had successfully found the route to Asia. He was **promoted** to **admiral**, rewarded with money, and given permission to take another voyage.

One year later, in 1498, Cabot **departed** again. This time he took five ships. Unfortunately, there were no great discoveries. Only one of John Cabot's ships made it back to England. The other four ships, their crew members, and John Cabot were never heard from again.

——— JOHN CABOT'S FIRST VOYAGE

- - - - - JOHN CABOT'S SECOND VOYAGE

JOHN CABOT

Directions: Read each question carefully. Darken the circle for the correct answer.

1 **John Cabot was the son of a –**

   A merchant
   B ship builder
   C dentist
   D sailor

2 **Which country had complete control over the trade with Asia?**

   F Spain
   G Portugal
   H England
   J Italy

3 **Why was finding a shorter, safer route to Asia important to explorers like John Cabot?**

   A Every country wanted to establish colonies in Asia.
   B The explorer that sailed to Asia first got to claim the entire area for himself.
   C The country that found the shortest and safest route to Asia could take control of the Asian trade.
   D No explorer had ever been to Asia before.

4 **According to the map showing routes to Asia, Portuguese explorers –**

   F followed Christopher Columbus's route
   G sailed from Greenland
   H sailed around the world
   J sailed around the tip of Africa

5 **Which country supported John Cabot's voyage to find a route to Asia?**

   A Spain
   B Portugal
   C England
   D Italy

6 **Which statement about John Cabot's first voyage is <u>true</u>?**

   F It was forced to return to England.
   G It successfully reached Asia.
   H John Cabot had complete support from his crew.
   J John Cabot's first voyage only made it as far as Greenland.

7 **During John Cabot's second voyage, he may have gone as far as –**

   A Iceland
   B Ireland
   C Newfoundland
   D Maine

8 **What can you learn from studying the map of John Cabot's first and second voyages?**

   F John Cabot sailed to North America during his first voyage.
   G During his second voyage, John Cabot sailed west from England.
   H During his first voyage, John Cabot sailed south from England.
   J John Cabot's first voyage was longer than his second voyage.

READING

Answers

1 Ⓐ Ⓑ Ⓒ Ⓓ   5 Ⓐ Ⓑ Ⓒ Ⓓ
2 Ⓕ Ⓖ Ⓗ Ⓙ   6 Ⓕ Ⓖ Ⓗ Ⓙ
3 Ⓐ Ⓑ Ⓒ Ⓓ   7 Ⓐ Ⓑ Ⓒ Ⓓ
4 Ⓕ Ⓖ Ⓗ Ⓙ   8 Ⓕ Ⓖ Ⓗ Ⓙ

the source

Think about the ways we learn about history. Reading books, seeing movies, looking at photographs, studying maps, searching the Internet, digging for bones, and holding pieces of pottery are some of the ways that we learn about the past.

There are two types of sources to help us learn about what happened in the past. Primary sources are recorded by people who were there at the time. If you have ever read a diary or an **autobiography**, then you were reading something that was written by the person who was actually recording the events and experiences as they were happening. Diaries and autobiographies are primary sources. Letters, interviews, photographs, original maps, bones, and pieces of pottery are other examples of primary sources because they give us "first-hand" knowledge of an event that took place in history.

Secondary sources are recorded by people after an event took place. Many books have been written about important historical events and people. A book written in 2005 about the life of Viking explorer Erik the Red is a secondary source because the author wasn't actually there to interview the famous explorer and can't give any "first-hand" knowledge. Movies, **biographies,** newspaper stories, and encyclopedias are other examples of secondary sources because they give us "second-hand" knowledge of events that took place in history.

You have just finished studying about New World explorers Leif Erikson and John Cabot.

In this activity, you will decide whether a source of information is a primary source or a secondary source. On the lines provided, put a "P" next to the primary sources and an "S" next to the secondary sources.

1. _____ A model of a Viking pirate ship on display at the library.

2. _____ The original map of Greenland, drawn by Leif Erikson himself.

3. _____ Artifacts from Newfoundland uncovered by archaeologists Helge and Ann Ingstad.

4. _____ A movie about famous Viking pirate Erik the Red.

5. _____ John Cabot's autobiography.

6. _____ John Cabot's letter to Portugal and Spain asking for support of his voyage to Asia.

7. _____ A photograph of Leif Erikson standing next to his first boat.

GIOVANNI DA VERRAZANO

Giovanni da Verrazano (vair•rot•SAH•no) was born in his family's Italian castle in about 1485. Not much is known about Verrazano's early life, but growing up in a wealthy Italian family meant that young Giovanni received an excellent education.

VERRAZANO THE PIRATE

In 1507, Giovanni da Verrazano moved to France. Like others you have read about, Giovanni da Verrazano wanted to navigate the seas and find a shorter route to Asia.

Verrazano's first voyages were across the Mediterranean Sea to the Middle East. He spent many years as a pirate, **raiding** Spanish and Portuguese ships.

He took nearly two million dollars worth of gold and jewels that the Spanish **conquistadors** (con•KEE•stah•dorz) had stolen from Mexico.

SAILING FOR FRANCE

In 1524, King Francis I of France chose Verrazano to search for a western route that would hopefully take him through North America to the Pacific Ocean and on to Asia. Verrazano was given two ships for his voyage. He set sail in January.

GIOVANNI DA VERRAZANO

New World Discoveries

On March 1, 1524, Verrazano reached Cape Fear in present-day North Carolina. He continued sailing north to explore the coastline. Verrazano believed he had found the Pacific Ocean. He had actually discovered Pamlico **Sound** in present-day North Carolina. Verrazano's mistake led mapmakers to draw maps that showed North America divided in two pieces, connected by a narrow strip of land. It took more than a **century** to correct Verrazano's error.

Verrazano continued north, discovering the New York Harbor, Block Island, and Narragansett (nar•ra•GAN•set) Bay. He claimed the entire area for France. He didn't sail close enough to the coastline to discover the Chesapeake and Delaware bays or the Hudson River. Before returning to France, Verrazano sailed to Maine and Newfoundland. Based on Verrazano's **journals**, historians believe that he **anchored** his ship at the exact spot in New York where the Verrazano-Narrows Bridge stands today.

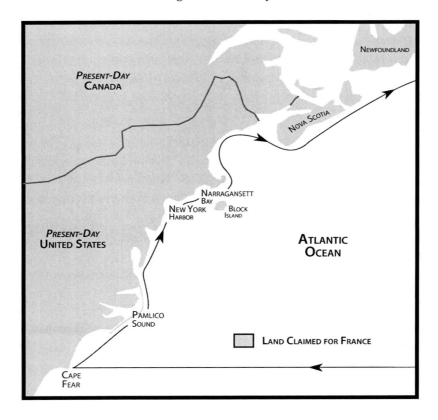

Verrazano's Other Voyages

Giovanni da Verrazano made two or three more voyages to the New World. In 1527, he explored Brazil. He was the first to cut logwood, an important tree whose leaves and bark are still used today for medical purposes.

In 1528, Verrazano explored Florida, the Bahamas, and islands in the **Caribbean**. While in the Caribbean, he anchored his ship away from shore and rowed a smaller boat to trade with the **natives**. It is not clear what happened next. Some believe that he was killed and eaten by **cannibals** of the tribe. Others think he died in 1528, during his third voyage to the New World. Another source believes that he was captured by Spanish conquistadors and hanged as a pirate.

Name _____

〰〰〰 GIOVANNI DA VERRAZANO 〰〰〰

Directions: Read each question carefully. Darken the circle for the correct answer.

1 **What do historians know about Giovanni da Verrazano's early life?**

   A The names of his friends.

   B The exact day and year of his birth.

   C The type of education that he received.

   D He grew up in a very poor family.

2 **When Giovanni da Verrazano grew up, he wanted to be a –**

   F navigator

   G merchant

   H trader

   J ship builder

3 **After reading about Verrazano's days as a pirate, you get the idea that –**

   A he only raided Spanish ships

   B he didn't make very much money as a pirate

   C he was taking money that had been stolen from someone else

   D he spent most of his time raiding ships in the Atlantic Ocean

4 **In what year did Verrazano first reach the New World?**

   F 1528

   G 1527

   H 1524

   J 1507

5 **When Verrazano reached Pamlico Sound in North Carolina, where did he think he was?**

   A Asia

   B The Pacific Ocean

   C The Gulf of Mexico

   D Canada

6 **It took more than a century to correct Verrazano's error. A <u>century</u> is a period of –**

   F 10 years

   G 50 years

   H 100 years

   J 1,000 years

7 **After studying the map of Giovanni da Verrazano's voyage, you learn that –**

   A he sailed to Nova Scotia first

   B after leaving Narragansett Bay, he sailed northeast

   C after reaching the New York Harbor, he continued south

   D he reached Pamlico Sound before reaching Cape Fear

8 **According to the map, the New York Harbor is located –**

   F north of Cape Fear

   G south of Pamlico Sound

   H northeast of Nova Scotia

   J southeast of Newfoundland

READING

Answers

1 Ⓐ Ⓑ Ⓒ Ⓓ   5 Ⓐ Ⓑ Ⓒ Ⓓ

2 Ⓕ Ⓖ Ⓗ Ⓙ   6 Ⓕ Ⓖ Ⓗ Ⓙ

3 Ⓐ Ⓑ Ⓒ Ⓓ   7 Ⓐ Ⓑ Ⓒ Ⓓ

4 Ⓕ Ⓖ Ⓗ Ⓙ   8 Ⓕ Ⓖ Ⓗ Ⓙ

～～ VOCABULARY QUIZ ～～
NEW WORLD EXPLORERS
PART II

Directions: Match the vocabulary word on the left with its definition on the right. Put the letter for the definition on the blank next to the vocabulary word it matches. Use each word and definition only once.

1. _____ admiral

2. _____ sound

3. _____ West Indies

4. _____ raiding

5. _____ journals

6. _____ North America

7. _____ promoted

8. _____ profits

9. _____ conquistadors

10. _____ Portugal

11. _____ Asia

12. _____ century

13. _____ navigators

A. one of seven continents in the world. Bounded by Alaska on the northwest, Greenland on the northeast, Florida on the southeast, and Mexico on the southwest.

B. a narrow passage of water between an island and the mainland.

C. the study of the stars and planets.

D. a journey for the purpose of exploring.

E. people who control the direction of a ship.

F. entering someone's property for the purpose of stealing.

G. cities or towns located next to water with areas for loading and unloading ships.

H. stories of a person's life written by someone else.

I. a buyer or seller whose goal is to make money.

J. Spanish soldiers who conquered the Native Americans of Mexico and Peru.

K. human beings who eat the flesh of other human beings.

14. _____ monopoly

15. _____ merchant

16. _____ Caribbean

17. _____ autobiography

18. _____ conflicts

19. _____ mariner

20. _____ investigate

21. _____ expedition

22. _____ departed

23. _____ biographies

24. _____ anchored

25. _____ astronomy

26. _____ cannibals

27. _____ ports

28. _____ natives

L.   the world's largest continent with more than half of the Earth's population.

M.   a chain of islands in the Caribbean Sea that stretches from the southern tip of Florida to the northeastern corner of South America.

N.   an arm of the Atlantic Ocean surrounded on the north and east by the West Indies, on the south by South America, and on the west by Central America.

O.   money made after all expenses have been paid.

P.   people who belong to a place because they were born there.

Q.   a country along the Atlantic Ocean on the southwestern edge of Europe whose capital is Lisbon.

R.   a period of 100 years.

S.   complete control over a product or service.

T.   a sailor who navigates a ship.

U.   the story of your life written by you.

V.   left an area.

W.   a naval officer of the highest rank.

X.   struggles or disagreements.

Y.   to examine carefully.

Z.   written records of daily events.

AA. moved up in rank.

BB. secured a boat so it wouldn't float away.

JACQUES CARTIER

Jacques Cartier (car•tee•YAY) was born in France near the end of 1491. Very little is known about Jacques Cartier's childhood. Historians believe that he may have discovered his love for adventure when he sailed with other French explorers to Newfoundland or Brazil.

CARTIER'S FIRST VOYAGE

In 1534, Cartier was given permission from the king of France to explore and find a western route to Asia. In the words of King Francis I, Cartier was "to discover certain islands and lands where it is said that a great quantity of gold and other precious things are to be found." Cartier wasn't the first explorer from France to search for a shorter route to Asia. Ten years before, in 1524, Giovanni da Verrazano (vair•rot•SAH•no) had sailed for France and claimed a large area of land in the New World.

On May 10, 1534, Jaques Cartier sailed from France. He followed Verrazano's route and explored parts of Newfoundland. Cartier sailed further and entered the Gulf of St. Lawrence. He sailed to Breton and Prince Edward islands and traded with the Native Americans he met in Chaleur (shu•LUR) Bay. Cartier planted a cross in the Gaspé **Peninsula** and named the entire area **New France**. He **kidnapped** two boys from an Iroquois (EAR•uh•kwoy) village who were fishing in the bay and took them back to France with him. Before leaving New France, he explored Anticosti Island. Cartier was certain that he had been to Asia. He had actually sailed to present-day Canada.

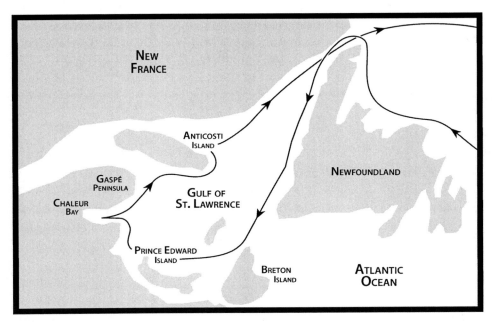

CARTIER'S SECOND VOYAGE

On May 19, 1535, Jaques Cartier left France with three ships, 110 men, and the two Native American boys that he had taken during his first voyage. Reaching the St. Lawrence River, he found the Iroquois village. The boys were **reunited** with their father, Chief Donnacona.

Cartier left his two largest ships in the harbor near the Iroquois village of Stadacona. He took his smallest ship and a few crew members up the river to a larger Iroquois village in present-day Montreal (mon•tree•ALL). More than 1,000 Iroquois came to greet Jacques Cartier and his crew. Today, the Jacques Cartier Bridge stands at that same spot in Montreal.

WINTER IN CANADA

Cartier and his crew returned to Stadacona where they stayed for the winter. They built a fort, collected firewood, and used salt to keep their fish and meat fresh. Jacques kept a journal about the Native Americans.

Cartier wrote that even during the coldest months of the winter when the ice on the St. Charles River was more than six feet thick, the Native Americans only wore leggings and **loincloths**.

During the winter at the Iroquois village, **scurvy** broke out. The disease took the lives of about 50 Native Americans and 25 of Cartier's men. More lives would have been lost if the Iroquois hadn't cured them with a mixture made from the bark and needles of the white cedar tree.

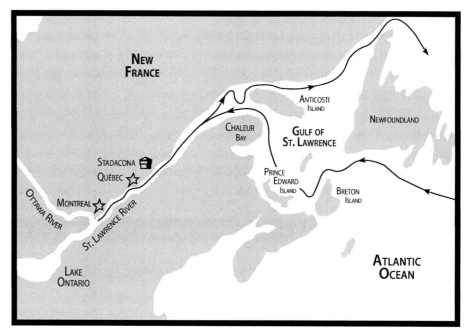

SAGUENAY (SAG•UH•NAY) KINGDOM

Chief Donnacona told Jacques Cartier about a village farther north that was full of gold, jewels, and other treasures. Cartier decided to take Chief Donnacona back to France with him so he could tell the king of France about this golden village known as Saguenay Kingdom.

On July 15, 1536, Jacques Cartier returned to France. Although he had not found the western route to Asia, he had claimed a large area of land for France. He also discovered the entrance to the St. Lawrence River and established friendly relationships with the Native Americans. The St. Lawrence River and the Native Americans would be very valuable for future expeditions and settlements in North America.

FRANCE'S FIRST NEW WORLD SETTLEMENT

On May 23, 1541, Jacques Cartier left on his third voyage to the New World. This expedition had nothing to do with finding a passage to Asia. Cartier was given five ships to find Saguenay Kingdom. He was also responsible for establishing a permanent settlement along the St. Lawrence River.

Three months later, Cartier arrived at the Iroquois village of Stadacona. There weren't as many Iroquois living in the village. In addition, the Native Americans weren't very happy to see him. Fearful for the safety of his settlers, Cartier sailed a few miles up the St. Lawrence River and built a French colony in present-day **Québec** (kwuh•BEK). The settlement was named Charlesbourg-Royal.

The 400 colonists at Charlesbourg-Royal built a village with homes and a fort for protection. They planted cabbage, turnips, lettuce, and built a shelter for the cattle they brought with them. The men of the colony began collecting what they thought were diamonds and gold. Two ships sailed back to France loaded with these treasures. They turned out to be worthless rocks.

JACQUES CARTIER

CARTIER RETURNS TO FRANCE

On September 7, 1541, Jacques Cartier left the colony to search for Saguenay Kingdom. He reached present-day Montreal before storms forced him back. When he returned to his colony, he found that the Iroquois had killed 35 colonists. In addition, scurvy broke out, taking even more lives. Instead of leaving again to search for Saguenay Kingdom, Cartier returned to France.

In 1543, Charlesbourg-Royal was **abandoned**. Disease, **harsh** weather, and **hostile** Native Americans forced the colonists to leave France's first settlement in the New World. It would be 65 years before another famous French explorer, Samuel Champlain (sham•PLANE), would build a permanent settlement in New France.

〰〰〰 JACQUES CARTIER 〰〰〰

Directions: Read each question carefully. Darken the circle for the correct answer.

1. If Jacques Cartier was born in 1491, how old was he when given permission from the king of France to find a western route to Asia?

   A 43

   B 57

   C 33

   D 27

2. Whose route did Jacques Cartier follow to the New World?

   F Christopher Columbus

   G Leif Erikson

   H John Cabot

   J Giovanni da Verrazano

3. By the end of his first voyage, Cartier thought he had sailed to –

   A Asia

   B Spain

   C Mexico

   D Canada

4. He had actually sailed to –

   F Asia

   G Spain

   H Mexico

   J Canada

5. What did Cartier take back to France with him?

   A Gold and silver that he had found.

   B Two Native American boys that he had kidnapped.

   C Spices, jewels, and rocks from Asia.

   D Plants and animals that he had found.

6. What can you learn by studying the map of Jacques Cartier's first voyage to New France?

   F Jacques Cartier sailed around the southeast coast of Newfoundland.

   G He sailed to Anticosti Island first.

   H Cartier sailed from Breton Island to Newfoundland.

   J Jacques Cartier entered and exited New France through the Gulf of St. Lawrence.

7. After reading about Jacques Cartier's second voyage to New France, you can conclude that –

   A the Native Americans were happy to see him

   B he arrived in New France by himself

   C Jacques and his crew returned to France before winter

   D the Iroquois were not willing to help Cartier's crew battle scurvy

8. Which statement about Jacques Cartier's third voyage to New France is <u>false</u>?

   F Cartier established a colony in Québec with 400 people.

   G The Native Americans welcomed the colonists with gifts.

   H The men of the colony thought they had found diamonds and gold.

   J Harsh weather and hostile Native Americans forced the colony to be abandoned.

READING

Answers

1 Ⓐ Ⓑ Ⓒ Ⓓ   5 Ⓐ Ⓑ Ⓒ Ⓓ

2 Ⓕ Ⓖ Ⓗ Ⓙ   6 Ⓕ Ⓖ Ⓗ Ⓙ

3 Ⓐ Ⓑ Ⓒ Ⓓ   7 Ⓐ Ⓑ Ⓒ Ⓓ

4 Ⓕ Ⓖ Ⓗ Ⓙ   8 Ⓕ Ⓖ Ⓗ Ⓙ

A time line is a tool used to list dates and events in the order that they happened. The time line below lists important dates in Jacques Cartier's voyages. Notice that many of the events are missing.

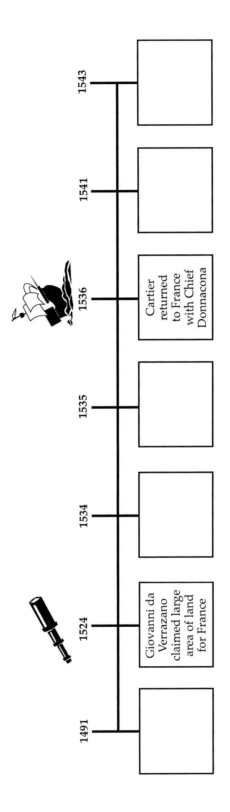

| 1491 | 1524 | 1534 | 1535 | 1536 | 1541 | 1543 |

Giovanni da Verrazano claimed large area of land for France

Cartier returned to France with Chief Donnacona

PART I

Directions: In the first part of this activity, you will use your information about Jacques Cartier to cut out and glue the missing events into the time line. Then, choose the picture that you think best represents each event. Color and cut out each picture before gluing it into its proper spot on the time line. Since you were not present for any of these events, this time line would be a **secondary source**.

| Cartier built Charlesbourg-Royal colony in Québec | Jacques Cartier was born in France | Native American attacks forced colonists to leave colony | Jacques Cartier sailed to New France on his second voyage | Cartier claimed land in present-day Canada for France |

Name _____

THAT
THAT

PART II

Directions: In the second part of this activity, you will create a time line of your life by listing the dates and events in order as they happened. Since you will be supplying the information about your own life, this time line would be considered a **primary source.**

1. Use the boxes drawn to make a time line of your life. Put the dates in the top boxes and the events in the bottom boxes.

2. The first date of the time line should be your birth. The last date should be the most recent event in your life.

3. Try to list only the important events. If you need more room, you may add more boxes on the back.

4. On a separate piece of paper choose one of the events from the time line and draw a picture of it.

SIR FRANCIS DRAKE

Sir Francis Drake was born in England. Most historians agree that the year of his birth was probably 1540. Francis was the oldest of 12 sons. His father was a farmer who later became a preacher. At the young age of 13, Francis went to sea on a **cargo** ship. He taught himself navigation skills. By the time he was 20, Francis was the master of the ship.

VOYAGES TO THE NEW WORLD

In the early 1560s, Francis Drake made his first voyages to the New World with his cousin John Hawkins. They sailed to West Africa, captured slaves, and sold them to Spanish farmers in the West Indies.

During one of their voyages, Drake and his cousin were attacked by a Spanish ship in the Gulf of Mexico.

The Spanish pirates took their ship and all of their slaves, but let Drake and his cousin escape with their lives. From that day forward, Drake hated the Spanish and made plans to get **revenge**.

In 1572, Queen Elizabeth gave Drake permission to work as a **privateer**, attacking Spanish ships and ports. Drake left England and sailed toward the New World with two ships and more than 70 sailors.

SIR FRANCIS DRAKE

Drake successfully attacked a Spanish ship carrying tons of gold from Mexico. He sailed back to England and presented Queen Elizabeth with the treasure. For his bravery, Queen Elizabeth **appointed** Drake as commander of an expedition to sail around the world.

Drake's Trip Around the World

On December 15, 1577, Francis Drake left England with five ships. Three of the ships were filled with more than 160 sailors. Two of the ships held all of the supplies for the voyage. Sailing through the Atlantic Ocean toward South America destroyed two of Drake's ships and claimed the lives of many of his sailors.

Drake sailed his three remaining ships through the **Strait of Magellan**, crossing from the Atlantic to the Pacific Ocean. Violent storms destroyed one of Drake's ships and caused another to return to England. A few weeks later, Drake's only remaining ship, the *Golden Hinde*, made it to the west coast of South America.

The crew sailed along the coast of South America towards Chile. Drake spotted Spanish ships carrying gold. He **plundered** the ships, taking all of their gold and supplies. A few months later, off the coast of Panama, Drake used the *Golden Hinde's* cannons to blow up another Spanish **vessel**. He found 80 pounds of gold, 26 tons of silver, and an unbelievable amount of pearls, jewels, and precious stones on the ship.

Claiming California

Francis Drake sailed on to present-day California and anchored his ship just outside of present-day San Francisco. Drake claimed the entire region for England. He spent the next year sailing toward home, making several stops along the way.

On September 26, 1580, the *Golden Hinde* sailed into England with Drake, 59 surviving crew members, valuable spices, and tons of Spanish treasure on board. He was the first Englishman to sail around the world. The leaders in Spain demanded that Queen Elizabeth have Drake **beheaded**. Instead, she honored Francis Drake by making him a **knight**. From that day forward, he was known as Sir Francis Drake. Once again, Queen Elizabeth put Sir Francis Drake in command of a **fleet** of English ships that continued to plunder Spanish ships and steal their gold.

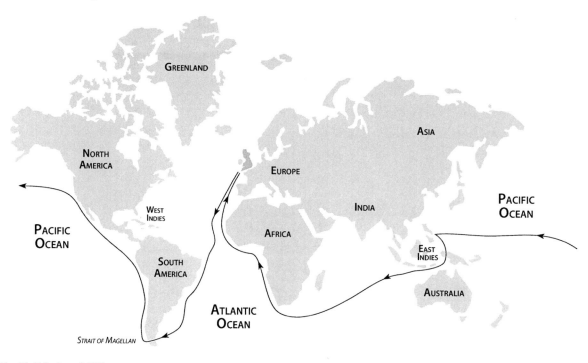

DEFEATING THE SPANISH

In 1585, Spain declared war on England. Sir Francis Drake led an attack on the Spanish port of Cadiz. He also stopped the Spanish **Armada** from **invading** the **English Channel**. In 1589, a year after **defeating** the Spanish Armada, Sir Francis Drake was sent to destroy more Spanish ships and take control of a cluster of islands off the coast of Portugal (POR•chuw•gal) known as the Azores. He destroyed a few ships, but lost 12,000 English lives and 20 of his own ships at the same time.

Sir Francis Drake's final years were spent doing what he loved best, finding and destroying Spanish ships. He died suddenly at the age of 56, while anchored off the coast of Panama. Sir Francis Drake was buried at sea in a lead coffin.

〰〰〰〰 SIR FRANCIS DRAKE 〰〰〰〰

Directions: Read each question carefully. Darken the circle for the correct answer.

1   **How many brothers did Francis Drake have?**

   A   12
   B   11
   C   10
   D   13

2   **After reading about Francis Drake's first voyages to the New World, you get the idea that –**

   F   he never made it to the West Indies
   G   some of Drake's best friends were Spanish pirates
   H   he was lucky to be alive
   J   Drake always sailed alone

3   **What can you learn by studying the map of the world on the bottom of the second page?**

   A   The East Indies are north of Australia.
   B   Greenland in southeast of Asia.
   C   The West Indies are in the Pacific Ocean.
   D   Africa is northwest of Europe.

4   **Which statement about Francis Drake's trip around the world is true?**

   F   He left for his voyage in the early 1600s.
   G   He sailed around the tip of South America instead of taking a shortcut through the Strait of Magellan.
   H   Only one of his five ships actually made it to the west coast of South America.
   J   Drake didn't find any gold or silver during his voyage.

5   **Besides claiming California for England, for what was Francis Drake most famous?**

   A   Plundering Spanish ships.
   B   Discovering the Strait of Magellan.
   C   Sailing around the world.
   D   Using cannons to blow up Spanish ships.

6   **Instead of beheading Francis Drake like the Spanish leaders demanded, Queen Elizabeth –**

   F   rewarded him
   G   threw him in prison
   H   took all of his ships away
   J   told Drake he could never sail again

7   **During Sir Francis Drake's defeat of the Spanish, which event happened first?**

   A   Sir Francis Drake died suddenly at the age of 56.
   B   Spain declared war on England.
   C   Sir Francis Drake stopped the Spanish Armada from invading the English Channel.
   D   Sir Francis Drake took control of the Azores Islands.

READING

Answers

1   Ⓐ Ⓑ Ⓒ Ⓓ   5   Ⓐ Ⓑ Ⓒ Ⓓ
2   Ⓕ Ⓖ Ⓗ Ⓙ   6   Ⓕ Ⓖ Ⓗ Ⓙ
3   Ⓐ Ⓑ Ⓒ Ⓓ   7   Ⓐ Ⓑ Ⓒ Ⓓ
4   Ⓕ Ⓖ Ⓗ Ⓙ

❧ Mapping: Cardinal and Intermediate Directions

Geography is the study of the Earth. It includes the Earth's land, water, weather, animal life, and plant life. **Geographers** are people who study geography. Sir Francis Drake was a famous geographer who sailed around the world and claimed a large part of California for England. You can think of yourself as a geographer because you will be learning about important places in present-day California.

Location is important to the study of geography. It is almost impossible to figure out your location or find your way around if you do not know the four main, or **cardinal directions.** North, south, east, and west are the **cardinal directions**. On a map these directions are labeled N, S, E, and W.

Compass Rose

Between the four main directions are the **intermediate directions.** Northeast, or NE, is the direction between north and east. Southeast, or SE, is the direction between south and east. Southwest, or SW, is the direction between south and west. Northwest, or NW, is the direction between north and west.

A **reference point** is also important for finding your location. A **reference point** is simply a starting point. It's difficult, for example, to travel east if you don't have a starting point.

Example: Channel Islands National Park provides underwater diving and protects **habitats** of many sea creatures. This includes the world's largest animal, the blue whale. Channel Islands National Park is located <u>southwest</u> of <u>Sequoia</u> (suh•KOY•yuh) <u>National Park</u>.

This example gives you some very important information. It tells you that your **reference point**, or starting point, will be Sequoia National Park. Locate Sequoia National Park on your California map. Put your finger on Sequoia National Park and slide it <u>southwest</u>. You should see a picture of Channel Islands National Park already placed there for you.

Sometimes directions contain more than one **reference point**. Look at the example below:

Example: Angel Island played a very important part in the history of the United States. It was once a Civil War camp, a gateway for soldiers returning from World War II, and a missile base. Today, a museum tells the story of Asian **immigrants** who came to the island. Angel Island State Park offers camping, biking, hiking and boating. Angel island state park is located <u>northwest</u> of <u>Yosemite National Park</u> and <u>south</u> of <u>Lassen Volcanic National Park</u>.

This example contains two **reference points** and two sets of directions. They have been underlined for you. Look at your map of California. Put your finger on Yosemite National Park and slide it <u>northwest</u>. Since there are many points of interest located northwest, a second **reference point** has been added to help you find your location.

The second **reference point** is Lassen Volcanic National Park. Place your finger on Lassen Volcanic National Park and slide it <u>south</u>. By using both of these **reference points**, you should be able to easily locate Angel Island State Park.

Directions: In this activity you will use reference points, cardinal directions, and intermediate directions to plot important points of interest on a California map. Many of these points of interest **preserve** history. This helps historians learn more about the people who lived before us.

1. Use your coloring pencils to color each of California's points of interest on the bottom of the last page.

2. Use your scissors to carefully cut out each point of interest.

3. Label the cardinal and intermediate directions on the compass rose drawn for you on the blank California map.

4. Use the written directions and your compass rose to correctly locate the points of interest on your California map.

5. To get you started, the reference points and directions have been underlined for you in the first five descriptions. You may want to underline the reference points and directions in the rest of the activity.

6. Glue the symbols in their proper places on your map. (Glue the symbols right over the dots.)

7. Use your coloring pencils to add color to the rest of your California map.

1. Lava Beds National Monument is the site of the largest number of lava tube caves in the United States. Lava tubes are tunnels that lava travels through. As the lava cools and hardens, a long, cave-like **channel** forms. During the Modoc War of 1872-1873, the Modoc people hid in the lava tubes for protection from the United States Army. Lava Beds National Monument is located <u>northeast</u> of <u>Lassen Volcanic National Park</u>.

2. Crystal Cove State Park is a 2,800-acre park with wooded canyons, open **bluffs**, and three miles of Pacific coastline. Mountain bikers, scuba divers, swimmers, and surfers enjoy plenty of activity at Crystal Cove State Park. Crystal Cove State Park is located <u>northeast</u> of <u>Channel Islands National Park</u> and <u>southeast</u> of <u>Sequoia National Park</u>.

3. Red Rock Canyon State Park was once home to Native Americans who left **petroglyphs** in the mountains. The park features desert cliffs, **buttes**, and spectacular rock **formations** that served as landmarks for wagon trains that stopped in the area for water during the 1870s. Red Rock Canyon State Park is located <u>southeast</u> of <u>Yosemite National Park</u> and <u>northeast</u> of <u>Sequoia National Park</u>.

4. Redwood National Park is home to coast redwoods, which are the tallest and oldest living trees on Earth. Coast redwoods can live up to 2,000 years and grow over 300 feet tall. At one time, there were more than two million acres of coastal redwoods in northern California. About 90% of these trees were cut down and used for building houses and other wooden structures. In 1968, Redwood National Park was established to preserve the remaining coastal redwoods. Redwood National Park is located <u>west</u> of <u>Lava Beds National Monument</u>.

5. Death Valley National Park covers more than two million acres and is home to the lowest and hottest place in the **western hemisphere**. At higher **elevations** in Death Valley National Park, the temperatures are much cooler and the mountains are snow covered. Thousands of plants and animals live in Death Valley National Park. Death Valley National Park is located <u>northeast</u> of <u>Crystal Cove State Park</u>.

6. The first people to live on Alcatraz Island were Native Americans. From 1934 to 1963, Alcatraz Island was used as a prison. After the prison closed, Native Americans from several different tribes once again claimed the island and tried to buy it from the United States government. The government refused to sell Alcatraz Island to the Native Americans. In 1971, police officers removed the remaining Native Americans from the island. Today, visitors can tour the famous prison. Alcatraz Island is located southwest of Yosemite National Park.

7. Disneyland is known as the Magic Kingdom and the Happiest Place on Earth. Disneyland was first opened in 1955. Today, it is a world-famous theme park that features eight magical lands where Mickey Mouse, Donald Duck, and the rest of the famous Disney characters roam. Disneyland features more than 50 family attractions. Disneyland is located southwest of Death Valley National Park and east of Channel Islands National Park.

8. Grizzly Creek Redwoods State Park was once a resting stop for horse-drawn stagecoaches. Today, the park offers swimming or fishing in the Van Duzen River and hiking through the forest of redwood trees. Grizzly Creek Redwoods State Park is located southwest of Redwood National Park.

9. Joshua Tree National Park covers almost 800,000 acres. Two deserts at different elevations come together to form Joshua Tree National Park. The "low" desert, known as the Colorado Desert, stretches across the eastern half of the park. The "high" desert, known as the Mohave (mo•HA•vee) Desert, **extends** across the western half of the park. Joshua trees live in the cooler and wetter Mohave Desert. Interesting rock formations in Joshua Tree National Park were formed millions of years ago when hot lava oozed from the Earth's crust and cooled while still beneath the Earth's surface. Joshua Tree National Park is located southeast of Death Valley National Park and east of Disneyland.

10. The San Diego Zoo is home to about 4,000 animals from all over the world. Visitors to the San Diego Zoo will be treated to **exhibits** with names like Gorilla Tropics, Polar Bear Plunge, Rain Forest **Aviary**, Reptile Mesa, and Absolutely Apes. Some of the world's rarest and most **endangered** plants and animals live in their natural habitats at the San Diego Zoo. The zoo takes great care to preserve these plants and animals and teach people how to protect them as well. The San Diego Zoo is located southeast of Disneyland.

Lava Beds
National Monument

Redwood
National Park

Grizzly Creek
Redwoods State Park

Alcatraz Island

Red Rock Canyon
State Park

Crystal Cove
State Park

Death Valley
National Park

Joshua Tree
National Park

Disneyland

San Diego Zoo

CALIFORNIA MAP

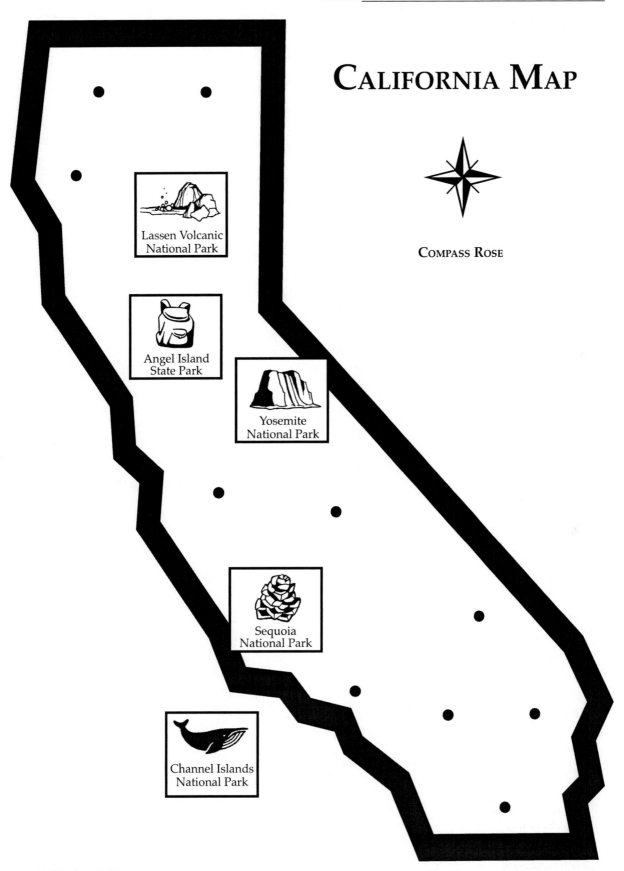

COMPASS ROSE

Lassen Volcanic
National Park

Angel Island
State Park

Yosemite
National Park

Sequoia
National Park

Channel Islands
National Park

~~~~ VOCABULARY QUIZ ~~~~
NEW WORLD EXPLORERS
PART III

Directions: Match the vocabulary word on the left with its definition on the right. Put the letter for the definition on the blank next to the vocabulary word it matches. Use each word and definition only once.

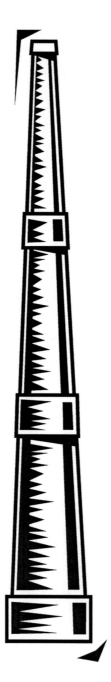

1. _____ vessel

2. _____ abandoned

3. _____ harsh

4. _____ hostile

5. _____ revenge

6. _____ appointed

7. _____ beheaded

8. _____ kidnapped

9. _____ loincloths

10. _____ privateer

11. _____ plundered

12. _____ New France

13. _____ peninsula

14. _____ bluffs

15. _____ petroglyphs

16. _____ knight

17. _____ invading

A.   gave up completely.

B.   arrangements of something.

C.   a large piece of land surrounded by water on three sides.

D.   cut off someone's head.

E.   pieces of cloth worn around the hips.

F.   took someone without permission.

G.   robbed.

H.   carvings or drawings in rocks usually made by people who lived a long time ago.

I.   in danger of disappearing forever.

J.   large boat.

K.   a building where birds are kept.

L.   displays.

M.   a long, narrow, deep part of a body of water.

N.   an owner of a private ship with weapons that are licensed to attack enemy ships.

O.   joined back together.

P.   an arm of the Atlantic Ocean that forms a waterway between France and Britain.

Q.   entering an area and taking it over by force.

18. _____ Québec

19. _____ immigrants

20. _____ habitats

21. _____ formations

22. _____ elevations

23. _____ reunited

24. _____ scurvy

25. _____ English Channel

26. _____ endangered

27. _____ Strait of Magellan

28. _____ exhibits

29. _____ extends

30. _____ western hemisphere

31. _____ aviary

32. _____ Armada

33. _____ channel

34. _____ buttes

35. _____ cargo

36. _____ defeating

37. _____ preserve

38. _____ fleet

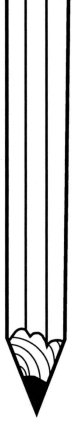

R. winning victory over.

S. steep riverbanks or cliffs.

T. to get even with someone for unfair treatment.

U. people who permanently settle in another country.

V. mounds of earth, much like mountains.

W. chosen or selected.

X. a narrow strip of sea that connects the Atlantic and Pacific oceans near the southern tip of South America.

Y. protect from injury or ruin so more can be learned.

Z. French colonies in North America from 1534 to 1763.

AA. large group of ships.

BB. heights to which things are raised.

CC. very uncomfortable conditions.

DD. the half of the Earth that contains North America, Central America, and South America.

EE. places where plants and animals grow or live in nature.

FF. angry and unfriendly.

GG. an honor given to a man who has done something very special for England.

HH. large group of Spanish warships defeated by the English Navy in 1588.

II. freight carried by a ship.

JJ. a disease caused from lack of vitamin C that results in swollen and bleeding gums, bleeding under the skin, and extreme weakness.

KK. the largest province in Canada.

LL. stretches.

SAMUEL DE CHAMPLAIN

Samuel de Champlain was born in France around the year 1567. As the son and nephew of ship captains, young Samuel received an education in navigation and mapmaking.

SAILING TO THE NEW WORLD

In 1603, Champlain sailed to New France as a **geographer** on a fur trading expedition. He used the information from this expedition to make excellent maps of the area.

In 1604, Champlain made a second trip to New France. Again, he was traveling with a fur trader who had been given complete control of the fur trade in New France. During this voyage, Champlain helped establish a settlement in the Bay of Fundy.

After a harsh winter on the island, the settlement was moved south to Port Royal.

Champlain spent the next three years exploring the Atlantic Coast from the Bay of Fundy down to Cape Cod. In 1607, he returned to France.

A year later, Samuel de Champlain returned to New France as commander of one of three ships.

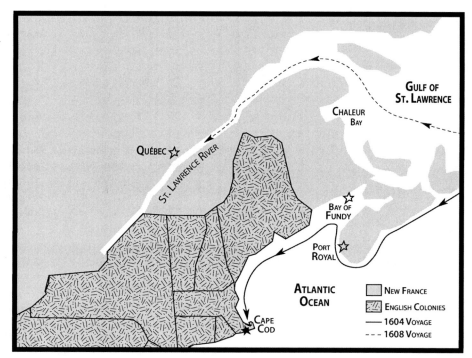

On July 3, 1608, Champlain sailed into the Gulf of St. Lawrence. He sailed around Chaleur (shu•LUR) Bay into the St. Lawrence River. He built a settlement in present-day Québec (kwuh•BEK) City with two story buildings and a **moat** that was 15 feet wide. The first winter in Québec was difficult for the colonists. Of the 28 people who arrived in 1608, only eight survived. Most died of scurvy, **smallpox**, or illness from the extremely cold weather in Québec.

THE IMPORTANCE OF THE FUR TRADE

Samuel de Champlain wasn't the only explorer working hard to build colonies in the New World. At the same time that Champlain was in Canada, English colonist John Smith was building the first of 13 English colonies in America. Building permanent settlements in the New World was very important to France and England. The country that controlled the most land also controlled the profitable beaver hunting and trading territories.

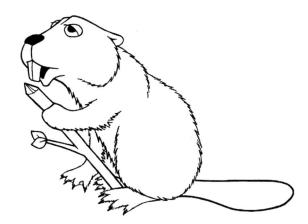

Beaver furs were worth a lot of money to the French and English colonists. The smooth, waterproof beaver furs were shipped back to France and England where they were sold for a very high profit. The French and English colonists would do anything to protect this business.

Building strong relationships with the Native Americans was also important to the colonists. It was the Native Americans who trapped the beaver and traded the furs for European goods, metal tools, and weapons. These were items the Native Americans had never seen before. Of course, all of the Native Americans wanted to trade with the colonists. There simply wasn't enough beaver for everyone to hunt and trade. Battles often broke out. The biggest and most organized tribes usually won.

NATIVE AMERICAN ALLIES

During the summer of 1609, Champlain focused on becoming **allies** with the Native Americans in New France. Tribes who spoke the Algonquian (al•GONG•kee•in) language lived in villages near the St. Lawrence River. The Algonquian agreed to ally with Champlain if he would help them defeat the powerful Iroquois (EAR•uh•kwoy) tribes who lived south of Québec.

Champlain gathered a small group of French soldiers and Native Americans. They sailed down the Richelieu (RISH•uh•loo) River to the body of water he named Lake Champlain. When they reached present-day New York, a battle broke out between Champlain's small army and a group of 200 Iroquois. Champlain fired his **musket**, killing two Iroquois with one shot. Afraid of the guns, the Iroquois turned and ran.

Champlain believed that the Iroquois could be easily defeated. Once the Iroquois were out of the way, the fur trade would be completely controlled by the French and their Native American allies. Champlain returned to France for more money and supplies. In the summer of 1611, he traveled to present-day Montreal (mon•tree•ALL) and began clearing the land for another French settlement.

CONTROL OF NEW FRANCE

In 1612, the king of France gave Samuel de Champlain full control over New France. Champlain was given the power to appoint leaders, make laws, sign **treaties** with the Native Americans, declare war, and remove unwanted people from New France. He was also responsible for finding gold and the easiest route to China.

FINDING A ROUTE TO CHINA

In 1613, Champlain explored the Ottawa River in hopes of finding the water route to China.

A year later, he sailed further up the Ottawa River and reached Lake Nipissing. Following the French River, he reached present-day Lake Huron.

BATTLING THE IROQUOIS

In 1615, Champlain set out on a **military** expedition to defeat the Iroquois and strengthen France's control on the fur trade.

His army paddled their canoes past Lake Ontario at its eastern tip. They hid their canoes and continued their journey by land. They followed the Oneida (oh•NIE•duh) River until they found themselves at an Iroquois fort in present-day New York.

Thinking the battle would be a quick one, Champlain's army attacked. Champlain was shot by arrows that wounded his leg and knee. Champlain and his men were forced to abandon the battle and **flee** the area. He realized that **conquering** the Iroquois would be more difficult than he once thought.

SAMUEL DE CHAMPLAIN

Fort Saint Louis

During the next winter, Champlain built Fort Saint Louis to protect his settlements in Québec. He worked on his relationships with the Native Americans and even signed an important peace treaty with the Iroquois tribes.

In 1628, English merchants raided Québec and took most of the village's supplies. England took control of New France and Champlain was taken to England as a prisoner. In 1632, France and England signed a treaty. Québec was returned to France and Champlain reclaimed his position as commander of New France.

Champlain spent the next year rebuilding Québec and establishing two other settlements in the area. Fearing that the Iroquois were allying with the English colonists, Champlain made plans to defeat the Iroquois once and for all.

Samuel de Champlain never got the chance to conquer the Iroquois. In October 1635, he had a **stroke**. Two months later, on Christmas Day, the man known as the Father of New France died.

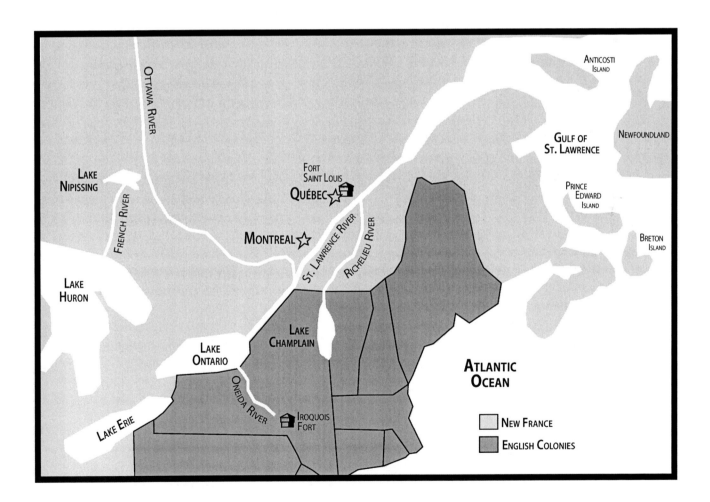

SAMUEL DE CHAMPLAIN

Directions: Read each question carefully. Darken the circle for the correct answer.

1 In 1603, Samuel de Champlain sailed to New France as a geographer on a fur trading expedition. A <u>geographer</u> studies –

A childhood diseases

B insects and bugs

C the Earth

D planets and stars

2 What can you learn by studying the map showing Champlain's voyages to New France in 1604 and 1608?

F During both voyages, he sailed into the Gulf of St. Lawrence.

G He reached Cape Cod during his voyage in 1608.

H Champlain sailed down the St. Lawrence River during his voyage in 1608.

J He sailed around Chaleur Bay in 1604.

3 According to the map, the Bay of Fundy is located –

A northeast of Cape Cod

B southwest of Chaleur Bay

C west of Québec

D north of the Gulf of St. Lawrence

4 After reading about the fur trade, you get the idea that –

F France controlled all of the land in the New World

G England controlled all of the land in the New World

H forming good relationships with the Native Americans was just as important as control of the land

J the English and French traders stole the beaver furs from the Native Americans

5 When Samuel de Champlain was given full control of New France, he was in charge of all of the following <u>except</u> –

A signing treaties with the Native Americans

B making laws

C building new colonies in New York

D declaring war

6 Which of the following is an example of a <u>primary source</u>?

F An encyclopedia article about Samuel de Champlain.

G A hat preserved from the 1600s that was made of beaver fur.

H Samuel de Champlain's biography.

J A report written about Samuel de Champlain by one of your friends.

7 According to the map on the last page, the French River –

A is located north of the Ottawa River

B empties into Lake Huron

C is located south of Lake Erie

D empties into Lake Champlain

8 Why didn't Samuel de Champlain ever get to conquer the Iroquois?

F England conquered them first.

G He was forced to return to France.

H He had a stroke and died.

J The Iroquois gave up without a fight.

READING

Answers

1 Ⓐ Ⓑ Ⓒ Ⓓ   5 Ⓐ Ⓑ Ⓒ Ⓓ

2 Ⓕ Ⓖ Ⓗ Ⓙ   6 Ⓕ Ⓖ Ⓗ Ⓙ

3 Ⓐ Ⓑ Ⓒ Ⓓ   7 Ⓐ Ⓑ Ⓒ Ⓓ

4 Ⓕ Ⓖ Ⓗ Ⓙ   8 Ⓕ Ⓖ Ⓗ Ⓙ

MAPPING: SAMUEL DE CHAMPLAIN'S VOYAGES

You have just finished reading about Samuel de Champlain's voyages to the New World. In this activity, you will draw Champlain's routes and label important land and water **resources** on a blank map.

Directions:

1. Using the blank map on the next page and your information about Samuel de Champlain, correctly label these islands and water resources. The lines have been numbered for you so you can easily see which islands and water resources need to be labeled. Spelling Counts!

ISLANDS	WATER RESOURCES
Anticosti Island	Atlantic Ocean
Breton Island	French River
Newfoundland	Gulf of St. Lawrence
Prince Edward Island	Lake Champlain
	Lake Erie
	Lake Huron
	Lake Nipissing
	Lake Ontario
	Oneida River
	Ottawa River
	Richelieu River
	St. Lawrence River

2. Choose two different coloring pencils. Use one to lightly shade in all of the land in New France.

   Use the other color to shade in the English Colonies.

   Use those same colors to shade in the boxes for New France and the English Colonies.

3. Draw in Champlain's route during his 1604 voyage and his 1608 voyage.

   Use a solid black line for his 1604 voyage.

   Use a dotted black line for his 1608 voyage.

Name

SAMUEL DE CHAMPLAIN'S VOYAGES

NEW FRANCE

ENGLISH COLONIES

1604 VOYAGE

1608 VOYAGE

HENRY HUDSON

Henry Hudson was born in England around the year 1570. As a young man in his teens, Henry worked as a cabin boy, running **errands** for the ship's captain and waiting on passengers and crew members. He worked his way up to captain, learning how to cook, sail, navigate, and read weather maps. As a captain, he was responsible for keeping a journal, so historians believe he was able to read and write.

Most of what we know about Henry Hudson's life came from his own journals and written records kept by his crew members during their four voyages with Henry Hudson.

HENRY HUDSON'S FIRST VOYAGE

In 1607, Henry Hudson sailed from England as the captain of his own ship, the *Hopewell*. He was trying to find a water route to Asia through the **North Pole**. Remember, finding a safe route to Asia was very important for Spain, France, and England. In Asia, they could buy jewels, silk, and spices that were not available in Europe. Hudson wanted to be the first explorer to find the important route to Asia.

During Hudson's first voyage, he sailed northwest from England along the coast of Greenland. He was only 700 miles from the North Pole. He did not find the passage to Asia. He did, however, sail farther north than any other explorer before him. He also discovered seals, walruses, and **pods** of whales on Spitzbergen Island in the Arctic

HENRY HUDSON

Ocean. This discovery would be important to English whale hunters in later years. In fact, Henry Hudson is often remembered as the grandfather of the whaling **industry**.

HENRY HUDSON'S SECOND VOYAGE

In 1608, just three months after returning from his first voyage, Henry Hudson was ready to sail again. This time he sailed northeast from England. He traveled as far north as the Nova Zembla islands in the Arctic Ocean. Huge pieces of ice blocked his way. Once again, he was forced to return to England without any information about a waterway to Asia.

After two unsuccessful voyages in search of a water route to Asia, England was no longer interested in supporting Henry Hudson's expeditions. Not willing to give up, Hudson turned to the Dutch, England's biggest trading **rival**.

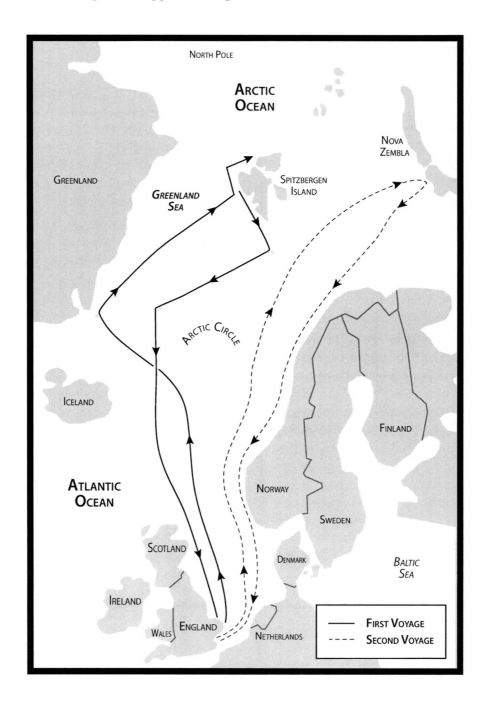

SAILING FOR THE DUTCH

In 1609, Henry Hudson left **Amsterdam** on his voyage for the Dutch. Instead of sailing north through the icy Arctic waters like he had done before, he sailed his ship, the *Half Moon,* west toward North America.

On July 12, 1609, the *Half Moon* sailed along the coast of Newfoundland in New France.

The crew continued sailing south, passing Nova Scotia. They reached the coast of present-day Maine where they were trapped in a thick fog for several days. After the fog lifted, Hudson and his crew went ashore and traded with the Native Americans.

Hudson continued sailing south, discovering Cape Cod, the Delaware Bay, and the Chesapeake Bay.

Before turning north, the *Half Moon* had sailed as far south as Virginia, where English colonist John Smith had recently founded Jamestown.

Hudson sailed up the Hudson River and claimed all of the land along the river for the Dutch.

The *Half Moon* anchored first in Albany and then off the northern tip of Manhattan Island in present-day New York. Both times, the crew went ashore to eat and trade with the Native Americans.

Henry Hudson planned to spend the winter in Newfoundland before searching again for a water route to Asia. His crew threatened to throw him overboard if he didn't take them home. On November 7, 1609, the *Half Moon* landed safely in England. Historians aren't sure why Hudson sailed to England instead of returning to Amsterdam.

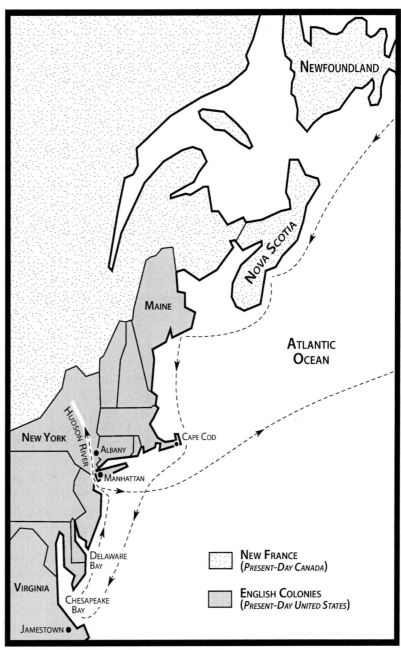

ARRESTED FOR TREASON

Less than a day after returning to England, Henry Hudson immediately made plans for a fourth voyage. Unfortunately, he wouldn't get the chance. He was arrested in England and found guilty of **treason** for sailing for the Dutch. He was held in England and never returned to Amsterdam. The Dutch were disappointed that Hudson had failed to find a safe water route to Asia, but they were excited about the land discoveries that Hudson had made in the New World. Dutch navigator Adriaen Block was sent to explore the new areas that Hudson had claimed for the Dutch. Block returned from his voyage with beaver furs and Native American **captives**. Block's explorations led to the first Dutch trading post in 1614, and New York's first permanent settlement in 1624.

HUDSON'S FOURTH VOYAGE

In 1610, Henry Hudson was released from jail. Though he had been found guilty of treason, England still wanted to find a water route to Asia. Since Henry Hudson was the explorer with the most experience, he was permitted to make a fourth voyage. This time, he sailed for England.

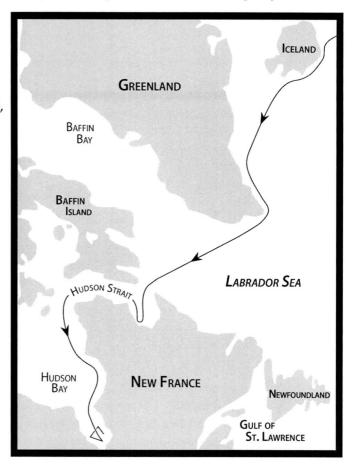

Shortly after dawn on April 17, 1610, the ship *Discovery* set sail from England. *Discovery* was loaded with crew and only eight months worth of supplies. Henry Hudson had difficulty with his crew from the beginning. There were constant fights between crew members and threats made against their captain, Henry Hudson.

A month later the crew reached Iceland. Bad weather and heavy fog forced them to stay in a safe harbor for another month. By June, Hudson and his crew sighted Greenland. They tried to land several times, but thick ice blocked the way. Strong winds and rough waters pushed the *Discovery* south and made many of the men sick. They sailed around the southeastern tip of Greenland and into a narrow area of water that was later named Hudson Strait.

As the *Discovery* sailed into the Hudson Bay, Captain Hudson mistakenly thought he had finally reached the Pacific Ocean. Ice formed on the water, forcing Hudson's crew to spend the winter in the southern end of the Hudson Bay. The crew suffered from cold, hunger, and disease. They were so angry with Hudson that they put him, his son, and a few of his crew members in a tiny boat and sailed away without them. The remaining crew members sailed the *Discovery* back to England. Henry Hudson was never seen again.

Name _____

Directions: Read each question carefully. Darken the circle for the correct answer.

1 **After reading the first paragraph about Henry Hudson, you can conclude that –**

   A he was a very lazy man

   B explorers who kept journals could read and write

   C he never became the captain of his own ship

   D he was born in the early 1500s.

2 **During his first voyage, Henry Hudson –**

   F sailed from France

   G found the water route to Asia through the North Pole

   H sailed farther north than any other explorer before him

   J sailed through the Pacific Ocean

3 **What can you learn by studying the map of Henry Hudson's first two voyages?**

   A Both voyages left from Greenland.

   B Only his second voyage sailed through the Arctic Circle.

   C Hudson's second voyage took him to Spitzbergen Island.

   D Henry Hudson was closer to Norway during his second voyage.

4 **While sailing for the Dutch, Henry Hudson discovered all of the following <u>except</u> –**

   F Cape Cod

   G the Chesapeake Bay

   H the Pacific Ocean

   J the Hudson River

5 **After spending the winter in Newfoundland, Henry Hudson planned to –**

   A search for the water route to Asia

   B stay in New France for a few years

   C kidnap Native Americans and take them back to Amsterdam with him

   D return to New York and build a Dutch colony

6 **Which phrase describes how his crew felt about his plans?**

   F ...went ashore to eat and trade with the Native Americans...

   G ...threatened to throw him overboard if he didn't take them home...

   H ...landed safely in England...

   J ...sailed as far south as Virginia, where colonist John Smith had founded Jamestown...

7 **Henry Hudson made his fourth voyage for –**

   A England

   B France

   C the Dutch

   D Italy

8 **According to the map on the last page, Henry Hudson's fourth voyage –**

   F ended north of Iceland

   G sailed through the Gulf of St. Lawrence

   H only made it to Greenland

   J ended west of New France

READING

Answers

1 Ⓐ Ⓑ Ⓒ Ⓓ   5 Ⓐ Ⓑ Ⓒ Ⓓ
2 Ⓕ Ⓖ Ⓗ Ⓙ   6 Ⓕ Ⓖ Ⓗ Ⓙ
3 Ⓐ Ⓑ Ⓒ Ⓓ   7 Ⓐ Ⓑ Ⓒ Ⓓ
4 Ⓕ Ⓖ Ⓗ Ⓙ   8 Ⓕ Ⓖ Ⓗ Ⓙ

SCALE MAPPING: GOING THE DISTANCE

Henry Hudson completed three voyages for England and one voyage for the Dutch. In all, he sailed more than 20,000 miles or 32,000 **kilometers**.

A map helps us track Henry Hudson's voyages by giving us a small view of a big place. It would be impossible to show 20,000 miles or 32,000 kilometers on a map that sits on your desk or fits on this piece of paper. Map makers use **scale rulers** to measure the long distances from place to place.

The **scale ruler** below can be used to measure the miles traveled by Henry Hudson. Then, with some quick multiplication, we can find out how many kilometers he traveled.

Each line on the ruler represents 30 miles traveled by Henry Hudson. Every ten lines on the ruler equals 300 miles. The 300-mile lines on the ruler have been clearly labeled. Laying the ruler along Henry Hudson's route drawn on a map will show you the distance that he sailed without ever leaving your classroom!

MEASURING USING A SCALE RULER:

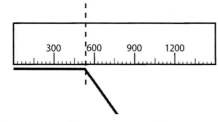

- To measure the route using the scale ruler, place the ruler on the route as shown above.

- Make sure you line up the end of the ruler with the end of the route.

- Since we are measuring in miles, and each small line equals 30 miles, this part of the voyage measures 540 miles.

THEN

- Turn the ruler so you can measure the next part of the route. Again, place the ruler as shown above.

- This part of the voyage measures 450 miles.

- Add both measurements to find the entire length of the voyage.

- 540 miles + 450 miles equals 990 miles.

The route is 990 miles long! How many kilometers is this? Every mile is equal to 1.61 kilometers. So, multiply 990 X 1.61 to find out how many kilometers were traveled.

$$
\begin{array}{r}
990 \\
\times \quad 1.61 \\
\hline
990 \\
+ \quad 59400 \\
99000 \\
\hline
1{,}593.90 \text{ kilometers}
\end{array}
$$

Directions: In this activity, you will use a scale ruler to measure the distance traveled by Henry Hudson during each of his four voyages.

1. Cut out the scale rulers at the bottom of the page. (Be careful not to cut off the front of the ruler as this will affect your measurements.)

2. Use your scale rulers to measure the distance that Henry Hudson traveled during each of his four voyages. Turn the ruler as shown in the example so you can measure each curve of the routes.

   Notice that the scale ruler is different for Hudson's third voyage. Each line on the ruler represents 20 miles. Every 10 lines on the ruler equals 200 miles.

3. On a separate piece of paper, add up the total number of miles traveled during each voyage. Put the correct answer in the box below the map.

4. Find out how many kilometers were traveled during each voyage by multiplying the number of miles by 1.61, just like in the example. Again, put the correct answer in the box below the map.

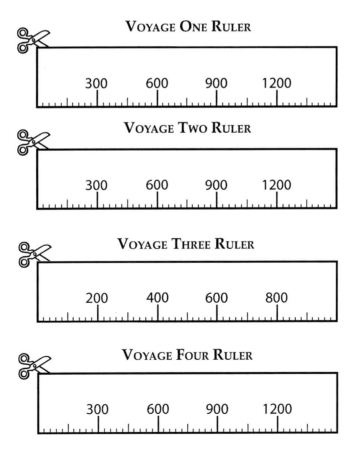

VOYAGE ONE

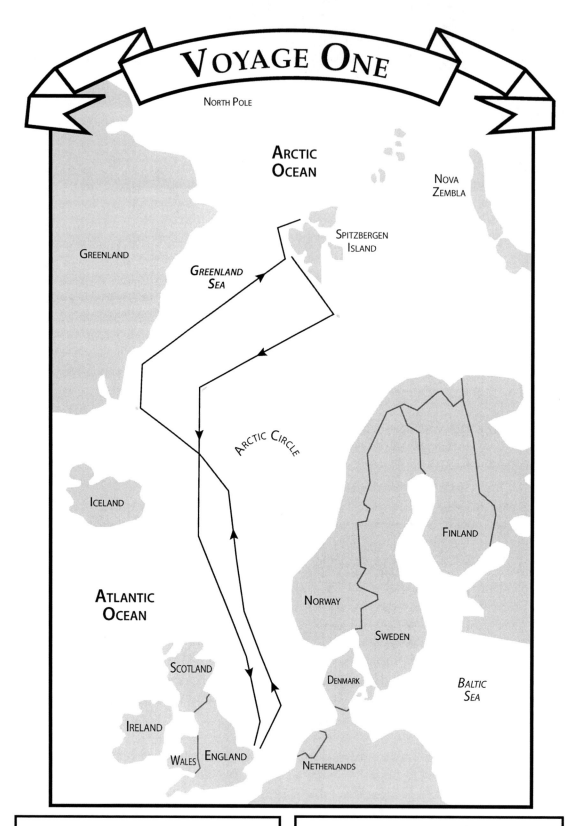

VOYAGE ONE MILES TRAVELED	VOYAGE ONE KILOMETERS TRAVELED

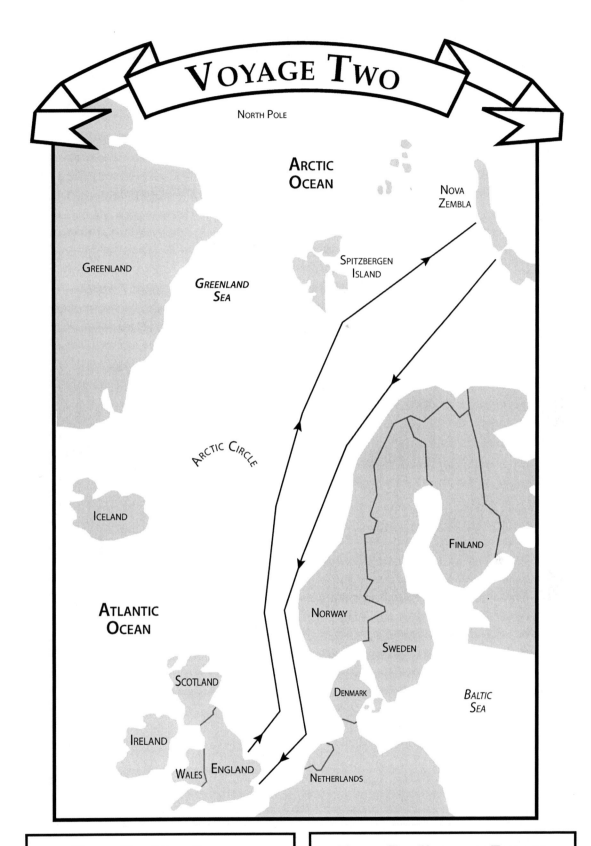

VOYAGE TWO

NORTH POLE

ARCTIC OCEAN

NOVA ZEMBLA

SPITZBERGEN ISLAND

GREENLAND

GREENLAND SEA

ARCTIC CIRCLE

ICELAND

FINLAND

ATLANTIC OCEAN

NORWAY

SWEDEN

SCOTLAND

DENMARK

BALTIC SEA

IRELAND

WALES ENGLAND

NETHERLANDS

VOYAGE TWO MILES TRAVELED	VOYAGE TWO KILOMETERS TRAVELED

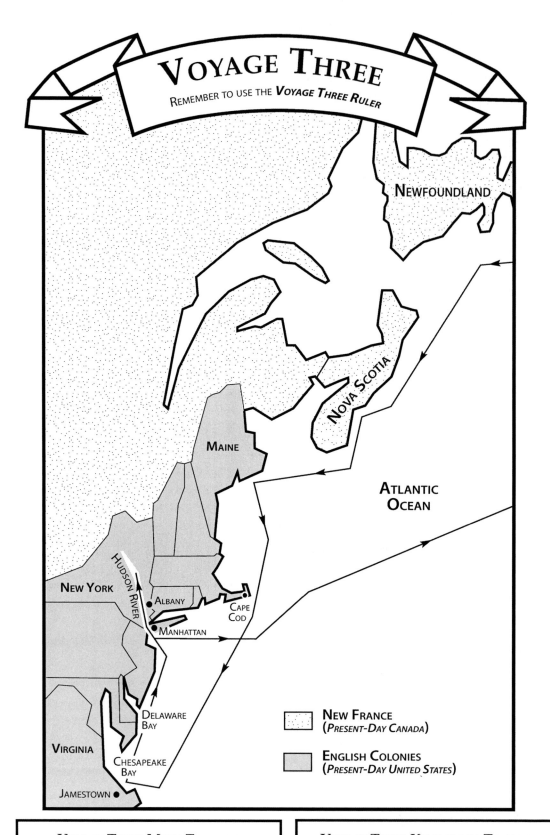

VOYAGE THREE

REMEMBER TO USE THE *VOYAGE THREE RULER*

NEWFOUNDLAND

NOVA SCOTIA

MAINE

ATLANTIC
OCEAN

HUDSON RIVER

NEW YORK

● ALBANY

CAPE
COD

● MANHATTAN

DELAWARE
BAY

☐ NEW FRANCE
(*PRESENT-DAY CANADA*)

▨ ENGLISH COLONIES
(*PRESENT-DAY UNITED STATES*)

VIRGINIA

CHESAPEAKE
BAY

JAMESTOWN ●

VOYAGE THREE MILES TRAVELED	VOYAGE THREE KILOMETERS TRAVELED

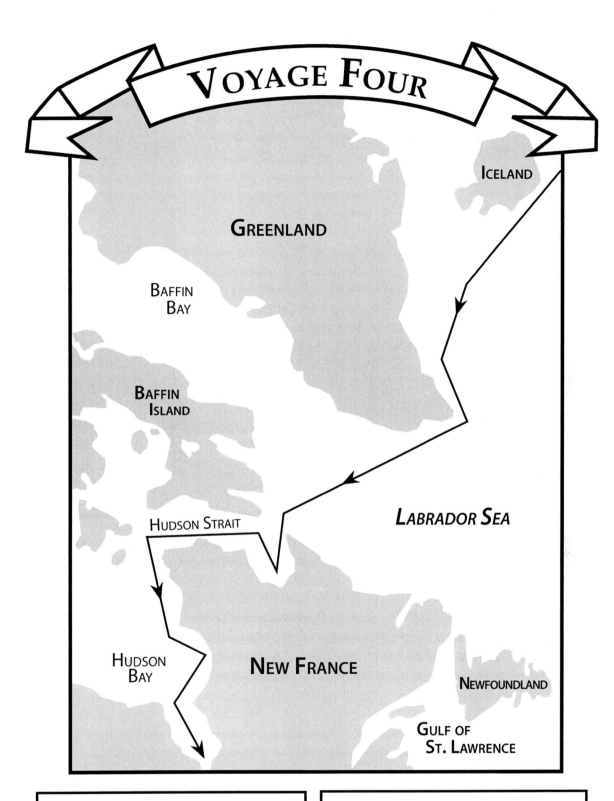

VOYAGE FOUR

ICELAND

GREENLAND

BAFFIN BAY

BAFFIN ISLAND

HUDSON STRAIT

LABRADOR SEA

HUDSON BAY

NEW FRANCE

NEWFOUNDLAND

GULF OF ST. LAWRENCE

VOYAGE FOUR MILES TRAVELED	VOYAGE FOUR KILOMETERS TRAVELED

ROBERT LA SALLE

Robert La Salle was born in France on November 22, 1643. As a child, Robert attended a school run by **Jesuit** (JEZ•ooh•wit) priests. His favorite subjects were science and nature. In 1660, at the age of 17, Robert took his **vows** and became a Jesuit priest. A few years later, he changed his mind and asked to be released from his vows.

ARRIVAL IN NEW FRANCE

In 1667, Robert La Salle traveled to New France. He planned to become a farmer. La Salle was given a large strip of land along the banks of the St. Lawrence River in Montreal (mon•tree•ALL).

The land that La Salle was given was in a very dangerous area. It was known for hostile Native Americans and harsh weather.

La Salle immediately started building a village and learning the Iroquois (EAR•uh•kwoy) language so he could communicate with the native people in New France.

The Iroquois told La Salle about a great river that led to the sea. La Salle was sure that this was the water route to Asia. Finding the water route would make him famous and give France complete control of the trade with Asia.

ROBERT LA SALLE

FAST FACTS

- Robert La Salle's full name was Rene-Robert Cavelier, Sieur de La Salle. Cavelier is a French word that means knight in English.
- La Salle chose to travel to New France because his brother, Jean, was a priest in New France.
- La Salle was so eager to find a water route to China that he spoke of nothing else. To make fun of him, his land in Montreal was nicknamed Le Chin. The name was later changed to Lachine.

La Salle's First Expedition

La Salle sold all of his land in New France and began making plans for his expedition. In 1669, he left Québec (kwuh•BEK) with five canoes and 12 men. He spent the next few years exploring. He traveled up the St. Lawrence River to Lake Ontario, going as far as Louisville in the Ohio River Valley. By the end of his journey, La Salle believed that the Mississippi River flowed south to the Gulf of Mexico.

La Salle spent the following year building a fur trading post on Lake Ontario. When the trading post was finished, he named it Fort Frontenac. This was in honor of Louis Frontenac, the **governor** of New France. In 1674, La Salle traveled to France. King Louis XIV gave La Salle control over the fur trade at Fort Frontenac and honored him with a title of **nobility**. Over the next five years, La Salle built Fort Niagara and other trading posts in the area and became a very wealthy fur trader.

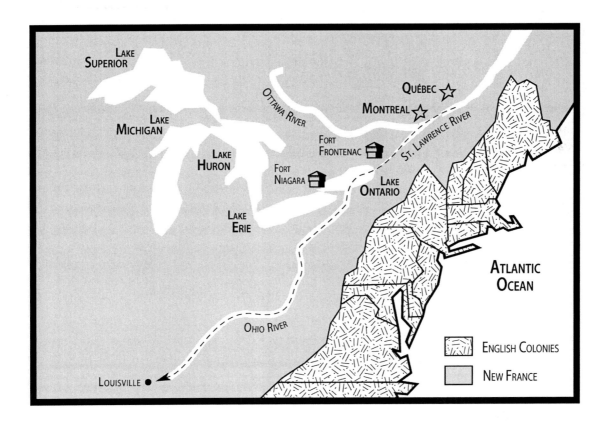

LOUIS JOLIET (JOE•LEE•ET) AND JACQUES MARQUETTE (MAR•KET)

Louis Joliet was a fur trader in New France looking for adventure. Father Marquette had been sent to New France to establish **missions** among the Native Americans. The pair met while working with Native Americans in the **Great Lakes** region. They had been told about the same river in the south that La Salle had searched for.

Like Robert La Salle, Joliet and Marquette hoped to become famous by finding the river that connected to the Pacific Ocean with the water route to Asia.

THE MISSISSIPPI RIVER

In 1673, France sent Louis Joliet to search for this mysterious river. Joliet chose Father Marquette to be the **missionary** for the expedition.

Five others, including Native American guides, joined them on their journey. They followed Lake Michigan to Green Bay and canoed up the Fox River. The group followed the Wisconsin River to the Mississippi River. They paddled down the Mississippi River and explored for hundreds of miles.

Joliet and Marquette soon realized that the Mississippi River only ran south, not east and west like they had hoped. Instead of connecting the Atlantic and Pacific oceans, the pair decided that the river flowed into

LOUIS JOLIET AND FATHER JACQUES MARQUETTE

the Gulf of Mexico. They journeyed as far as the Arkansas River, but they were warned that if they went farther they would meet hostile Native Americans and Spanish traders. Afraid for their safety, the group turned back toward Lake Michigan. Although they did not find the water route to Asia, they did find the Mississippi River and an area that was full of fish and beaver furs.

LA SALLE'S SECOND EXPEDITION

After hearing about Joliet and Marquette's expedition, La Salle became interested in making a journey of his own. King Louis XIV gave La Salle permission to leave New France, claim land, build forts, and explore the area between Florida and Mexico. In 1679, La Salle set sail from New France on his ship, *Le Griffon*. La Salle and his crew sailed up Lake Erie to Lake Huron and then to Green Bay, Wisconsin. They continued exploring Lake Michigan by canoe, stopping for a short time to build Fort Miami.

The Father of Waters

By 1680, La Salle's party had traveled down the Illinois River and reached Illinois. Native Americans in the area told La Salle and his men horror stories about the Mississippi River. To the Native Americans, it was known as the "Father of Waters." Those who dared to enter the river with its dangerous **whirlpools** and poisonous monsters never returned. Afraid for their lives, many of La Salle's men refused to continue with him to the Mississippi River. Saddened by their lack of courage, La Salle built Fort Heartbreak.

In January 1682, La Salle and his remaining crew of 41 men sailed south down the Illinois River and entered the "Father of Waters." By February, they had reached present-day Memphis, Tennessee. Again, the area was claimed for France and Fort Prud'homme was built.

On April 6, 1682, La Salle and his men reached the Gulf of Mexico. A cross was planted in the ground and the land was claimed for France. In honor of King Louis XIV, La Salle named the entire region Louisiana. Louisiana was a huge area of New France that extended east to west from the Appalachian (ap•uh•LAY•shun) Mountains to the Rocky Mountains. From north to south, Louisiana stretched from the Great Lakes to the Gulf of Mexico.

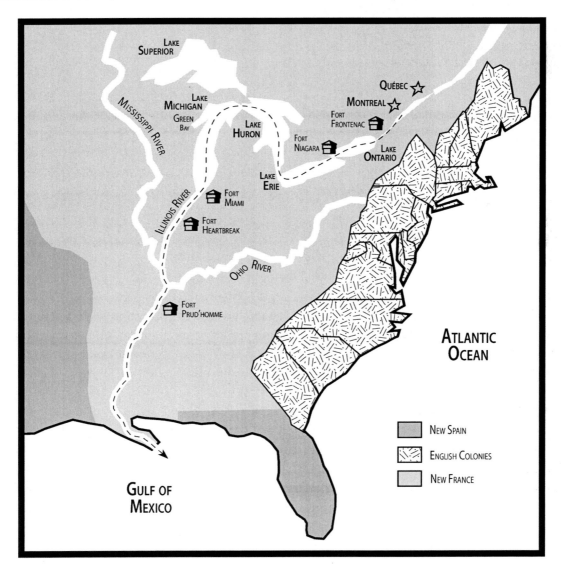

BUILDING A FRENCH COLONY

King Louis XIV gave La Salle permission to establish a French colony at the mouth of the Mississippi River. In 1683, La Salle sailed to France to pick up supplies and settlers for his colony.

The following year, La Salle set sail for the Gulf of Mexico with four ships and 300 colonists. The group included both men and women.

La Salle and his colonists weren't sure exactly where they were going. They just knew that they needed to sail across the Atlantic Ocean, through the Caribbean Sea, and into the Gulf of Mexico.

The colonists never reached the Mississippi River. One ship was captured by pirates in the West Indies. Another sank to the bottom of the ocean. The third ship got stuck in the mud off the coast of Texas.

FORT SAINT LOUIS

Poorly made maps and stormy weather caused the remaining ship to sail off course and completely miss the opening to the Mississippi River. It landed west of the Mississippi River near the present-day state of Texas. The colonists settled in Texas and built Fort Saint Louis right on the edge of Spanish territory.

ROBERT LA SALLE'S DEATH

Fort Saint Louis was under constant attack by Native Americans. Sickness, shortage of supplies, and lack of clean drinking water caused the death of many of Fort Saint Louis's colonists. By 1687, there were only 36 colonists left at Fort Saint Louis. Fearing that the entire colony would be lost, La Salle and several men started walking to find the Mississippi River. They planned to follow the river to New France and bring back more supplies. The group got lost and could not find the Mississippi River. Angry with their leader, Robert La Salle was murdered by his own men.

Name _____

≈≈≈≈≈ ROBERT LA SALLE ≈≈≈≈≈

Directions: Read each question carefully. Darken the circle for the correct answer.

1 Before traveling to New France, Robert La Salle was a –

A farmer

B fur trader

C navigator

D priest

2 During La Salle's first expedition in New France, all of the following events happened <u>except</u> –

F he traveled up the St. Lawrence River to Lake Ontario

G he reached the Gulf of Mexico

H he left from Québec

J he traveled with 12 men in five canoes

3 Why was Father Jacques Marquette sent to New France?

A To find a water route to Asia.

B To establish missions among the Native Americans.

C To arrest Robert La Salle and take him back to France.

D To search for Louis Joliet.

4 In Joliet and Marquette's search for the Mississippi River, which event happened <u>second</u>?

F They sailed as far as the Arkansas River.

G They turned back toward Lake Michigan.

H They paddled down the Mississippi River and explored for hundreds of miles.

J They followed the Wisconsin River to the Mississippi River.

5 Why did many of Robert La Salle's men refuse to sail down the Mississippi River with him?

A They were told that the river was filled with poisonous monsters.

B They were afraid of Robert La Salle.

C They didn't want to see the Gulf of Mexico.

D The boat wasn't big enough to hold all of them.

6 What can you learn by studying the map of Robert La Salle's journey down the Mississippi River?

F His crew never made it to the Gulf of Mexico.

G The journey started in Québec.

H They traveled through Lake Superior.

J Fort Heartbreak was the last fort built before entering the Mississippi River.

7 Which of the following is an example of a <u>secondary source</u>?

A A piece of Robert La Salle's curly hair.

B Wood from Fort Frontenac.

C Joliet and Marquette's canoe preserved in a Canadian museum.

D A story written about La Salle's voyages.

8 How did Robert La Salle die?

F He was killed by Native Americans.

G He drowned in the Mississippi River.

H He was murdered by his own men.

J He was bitten by a rattlesnake.

READING

Answers

1	Ⓐ	Ⓑ	Ⓒ	Ⓓ	**5**	Ⓐ	Ⓑ	Ⓒ	Ⓓ
2	Ⓕ	Ⓖ	Ⓗ	Ⓙ	**6**	Ⓕ	Ⓖ	Ⓗ	Ⓙ
3	Ⓐ	Ⓑ	Ⓒ	Ⓓ	**7**	Ⓐ	Ⓑ	Ⓒ	Ⓓ
4	Ⓕ	Ⓖ	Ⓗ	Ⓙ	**8**	Ⓕ	Ⓖ	Ⓗ	Ⓙ

Name _____

FAMOUS Explorers

K·W·L·H CHART

Many brave explorers once risked their lives for fame and fortune. In this activity you will use **primary** and **secondary sources** to research one of the explorers you have learned about. Choose from Leif Erikson, John Cabot, Giovanni da Verrazano, Jacques Cartier, Sir Francis Drake, Samuel de Champlain, Henry Hudson, and Robert La Salle. Answer the questions below to get you started. Then use the charts on the next two pages to record your information.

1   Which explorer did you choose? _____

2   Why did this explorer set out on his voyage to the New World? _____
_____

3   Describe one challenge that this explorer faced in the New World. _____
_____

4   How did this explorer solve his problems? _____
_____
_____

DIRECTIONS:

1. Use the "What I Know" column of the charts on the next two pages to list facts that you already know about the explorer.

2. Use the "What I Want to Know" column of the charts to list five questions that you still have about the explorer.

3. Use books, encyclopedias, the Internet, and other sources to research and answer your questions. Write your answers in the "What I Learned" column of the charts.

4. List the book titles, encyclopedias, and website addresses that you used to find your information in the "How I Found Out" column of the charts.

5. Put a "P" next to the **primary sources** and an "S" next to the **secondary sources** that you used to find your information.

WHAT I KNOW	WHAT I WANT TO KNOW	WHAT I LEARNED	HOW I FOUND OUT	P / S

P/S			
HOW I FOUND OUT			
WHAT I LEARNED			
WHAT I WANT TO KNOW			
WHAT I KNOW			

Let's Talk About Famous Explorers

Now that you have finished your research and filled in the K•W•L•H Chart for one of the explorers, let's talk about what you have learned. Read the questions below and write your answers on the lines provided. Attach a separate piece of paper if you need more room. Be ready to discuss some of your answers.

1   Based on your research, what is the most important <u>new</u> detail that you learned about the explorer you chose?

_____

_____

2   Did your research change the way you thought about this explorer? Explain your answer.

_____

_____

3   Describe one important contribution that this explorer made to the New World.

_____

_____

_____

4   Is this contribution still important to us today? Explain your answer.

_____

_____

_____

THE FUTURE OF NEW FRANCE

By 1689, England had established most of its 13 original colonies along the Atlantic Coast. France controlled Canada, Louisiana, and most of the land in the Great Lakes region. Both countries claimed the Ohio River Valley.

THE OHIO RIVER VALLEY

The Ohio River Valley was rich in natural resources that included **fertile** farm land and plenty of water. Most importantly, the Ohio River Valley was full of beaver. The Iroquois (EAR•uh•kwoy) controlled the beaver hunting territories in the Ohio River Valley.

They had permitted some English colonists to settle in the Ohio River Valley. This made the French very angry.

The French believed that they controlled the fur trade with the Iroquois. To strengthen their claims on the area, both countries began building forts in the Ohio River Valley. Soldiers were trained. The French and English colonists were ready to protect their land.

During the next 70 years, the French and English colonists battled for complete

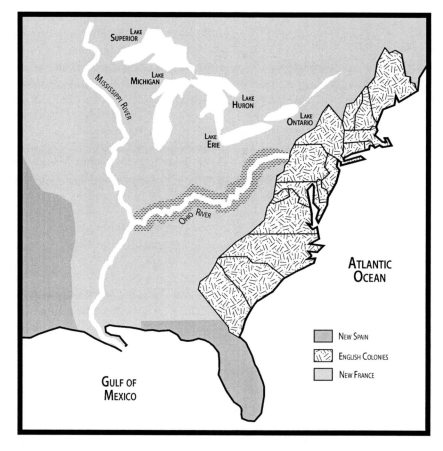

control of the Ohio River Valley. The last battle between France and England started in 1754. It was known as the French and Indian War.

THE FRENCH AND INDIAN WAR

In the beginning of the French and Indian War, large groups of French soldiers easily defeated small armies of English colonists. English forts were captured by the French and hundreds of English colonists were killed. It looked as if France might finally take control of the Ohio River Valley and the rest of England's land in North America.

In 1755, **Great Britain** sent 1,000 British soldiers to the Ohio River Valley. Still, the French and their Native American allies easily won several important battles. English settlements across the Ohio River Valley were raided. The Native Americans **scalped** the colonists, kidnapped prisoners, and burned their homes to the ground.

The English colonists fought back. A reward was offered for the scalp of every Native American male over the age of 12 years old. Great Britain sent money and supplies to build dozens of forts to protect its colonists. In 1758, more than 8,000 British soldiers were sent to help the colonists battle the French and their Native American allies.

DEFEATING THE FRENCH

Beginning in 1758, the French found themselves **outnumbered** by British troops and the colonists' **militias** (muh•LIH•shuz). France turned to Spain for help. Spanish soldiers were sent in to fight. Even with Spain's help, the British troops were successful in many battles.

In the fall of 1759, a large army of British soldiers invaded Canada in New France. They took over the city of Québec. A year later, the city of Montreal (mon•tree•ALL) was also captured by the British Army. Fearing complete defeat, France and its Native American allies **surrendered**.

THE TREATY OF PARIS

In 1763, the French and Indian War officially ended with the Treaty of Paris. The treaty was signed by Great Britain, France, and Spain. France gave all of its land in New France east of the Mississippi River, except for New Orleans, to Great Britain.

Great Britain also received most of France's land in Canada.

Control of the five Great Lakes and all of the valuable hunting territories now belonged to Great Britain. The treaty also required Spain to give its territory in Florida to Great Britain. In return for helping them during the war, France gave New Orleans and its territory west of the Mississippi River to Spain. France would never again control so much land in North America.

Name _____

THE FUTURE OF NEW FRANCE

Directions: Read each question carefully. Darken the circle for the correct answer.

1 **Which two countries claimed control of the Ohio River Valley?**

 A England and Spain

 B France and Italy

 C Spain and France

 D England and France

2 **According to the information you have read, what was the most important resource in the Ohio River Valley?**

 F Friendly Native Americans lived there.

 G There was plenty of water and fertile farm land.

 H The Ohio River Valley was full of beaver.

 J It connected to the Mississippi River.

3 **Which Native American tribe controlled the hunting territories in the Ohio River Valley?**

 A The Iroquois

 B The Huron

 C The Cherokee

 D The Algonquian

4 **According to the map of the Ohio River Valley, the English colonies were located –**

 F west of the Mississippi River

 G east of the Ohio River Valley

 H west of Lake Ontario

 J east of the Atlantic Ocean

5 **In the beginning of the French and Indian War, it looked as if _____ might win.**

 A France

 B Spain

 C England

 D Portugal

6 **How did Great Britain help the English colonists win the French and Indian War?**

 F Great Britain sent money, supplies, and soldiers.

 G Great Britain wrote letters to France's leaders telling them to stop fighting.

 H Native Americans were sent from Great Britain to help fight the war.

 J Great Britain convinced Spain to help fight the French and their Native American allies.

7 **According to the Treaty of Paris, which country received most of France's land in Canada?**

 A Spain

 B Great Britain

 C France

 D All of the above.

8 **According to the Treaty of Paris map, Spain controlled all of the land –**

 F east of the Mississippi River

 G in the 13 original colonies

 H north of the Great Lakes

 J west of the Mississippi River

READING

Answers

1 Ⓐ Ⓑ Ⓒ Ⓓ   5 Ⓐ Ⓑ Ⓒ Ⓓ
2 Ⓕ Ⓖ Ⓗ Ⓙ   6 Ⓕ Ⓖ Ⓗ Ⓙ
3 Ⓐ Ⓑ Ⓒ Ⓓ   7 Ⓐ Ⓑ Ⓒ Ⓓ
4 Ⓕ Ⓖ Ⓗ Ⓙ   8 Ⓕ Ⓖ Ⓗ Ⓙ

Name _____

～～～ VOCABULARY QUIZ ～～～
NEW WORLD EXPLORERS
PART IV

Directions: Match the vocabulary word on the left with its definition on the right. Put the letter for the definition on the blank next to the vocabulary word it matches. Use each word and definition only once.

1. _____ allies

2. _____ fertile

3. _____ governor

4. _____ Amsterdam

5. _____ conquering

6. _____ captives

7. _____ Great Lakes

8. _____ militias

9. _____ Jesuit

10. _____ errands

11. _____ flee

12. _____ Great Britain

13. _____ missionary

14. _____ industry

15. _____ geographer

16. _____ outnumbered

A. short trips to deliver messages or important documents.

B. a disease that can be easily spread to other people, causing fever, weakness, and puss filled bumps that usually leave scars.

C. a person sent to spread a religious faith.

D. rich soil that produces a large number of crops.

E. the capital of the Netherlands.

F. prisoners who have been taken by force without permission.

G. gave up.

H. having more people on one side than the other.

I. the northernmost end of the Earth.

J. a heavy gun used by soldiers, especially during the 1500s and 1600s.

K. groups of people who come together to help one another in times of trouble.

L. a deep ditch filled with water built to protect the entrance to a town or castle.

M. five large lakes located in North America at the border between Canada and the United States. The names of the lakes are Superior, Michigan, Huron, Erie, and Ontario.

17. _____ missions

18. _____ kilometers

19. _____ military

20. _____ North Pole

21. _____ nobility

22. _____ scalped

23. _____ vows

24. _____ pods

25. _____ moat

26. _____ rival

27. _____ whirlpools

28. _____ surrendered

29. _____ treason

30. _____ musket

31. _____ resources

32. _____ small pox

33. _____ stroke

34. _____ treaties

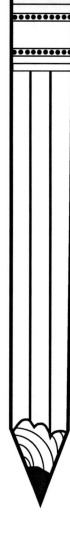

N.   an honor given to a person who has done great things for his country.

O.   business that provides a certain product or service.

P.   promises.

Q.   fast currents of water that move in a swirling motion.

R.   units of length that are equal to .621 of a mile.

S.   formal agreements.

T.   groups of seals, whales, or dolphins.

U.   cut the top of a human head that is usually covered with hair.

V.   groups of men having some military training who are called upon only in emergencies.

W.   defeating by force.

X.   a crime against your country's government.

Y.   things found in nature that are valuable to humans.

Z.   enemy.

AA. a scientist who studies the Earth's surface.

BB. people who are part of the armed forces who may be asked to go to war.

CC. a brain injury caused when a blood vessel bursts or is blocked.

DD. a person who is in charge of an area or group.

EE. the largest island in Europe. It includes England, Scotland, and Wales.

FF. churches.

GG. a part of the Catholic church known as the Society of Jesus.

HH. to leave quickly because of fear or danger.

GLOSSARY

A.D. the period in history after the birth of Jesus Christ.

a•ban•doned gave up completely.

ac•cused blamed or charged with a crime.

ad•mi•ral a naval officer of the highest rank.

al•lies groups of people who come together to help one another in times of trouble.

Am•ster•dam the capital of the Netherlands.

an•chored secured a boat so it wouldn't float away.

ap•point•ed chosen or selected.

ar•chae•ol•o•gists scientists who study past human life by looking at prehistoric fossils and tools.

Ar•ma•da large group of Spanish warships defeated by the English Navy in 1588.

ar•ti•facts objects and tools used by early humans for eating, cooking, and hunting.

A•sia the world's largest continent with more than half of the Earth's population.

as•tron•o•my the study of the stars and planets.

au•to•bi•og•ra•phy the story of your life written by you.

a•vi•ar•y a building where birds are kept.

bar•ren empty; unable to produce any crops.

bay a body of water surrounded by land that opens to the sea.

be•head•ed cut off someone's head.

bi•og•ra•phies stories of a person's life written by someone else.

bluffs steep riverbanks or cliffs.

buttes mounds of earth, much like mountains.

can•ni•bals human beings who eat the flesh of other human beings.

cap•tives prisoners who have been taken by force without permission.

car•go freight carried by a ship.

Ca•rib•be•an an arm of the Atlantic Ocean surrounded on the north and east by the West Indies, on the south by South America, and on the west by Central America.

cen•tu•ry a period of 100 years.

chan•nel a long, narrow, deep part of a body of water.

cli•mate the average weather conditions of an area over a period of years.

coast an area of land that borders water.

col•o•nists people who are ruled by another country.

con•flicts struggles or disagreements.

con•quer•ing defeating by force.

con•quis•ta•dors Spanish soldiers who conquered the Native Americans of Mexico and Peru.

con•vinced talked someone into doing something your way.

de•feat•ing winning victory over.

de•part•ed left an area.

el•e•va•tions heights to which things are raised.

en•dan•gered in danger of disappearing forever.

Eng•lish Chan•nel an arm of the Atlantic Ocean that forms a waterway between France and Britain.

er•rands short trips to deliver messages or important documents.

Eu•rope the sixth smallest of Earth's seven continents.

ex•hib•its displays.

ex•pe•di•tion a journey for the purpose of exploring.

ex•tends stretches.

fer•tile rich soil that produces a large number of crops.

flee to leave quickly because of fear or danger.

fleet large group of ships.

for•eign from another country or nation.

for•ma•tions arrangements of something.

found•ed started or established.

ge•og•ra•pher a scientist who studies the Earth's surface.

gla•ciers large bodies of ice moving slowly down a valley or spreading across the surface of the land.

gov•er•nor a person who is in charge of an area or group.

Great Bri•tain the largest island in Europe. It includes England, Scotland, and Wales.

Great Lakes five large lakes located in North America at the border between Canada and the United States. The names of the lakes are Superior, Michigan, Huron, Erie, and Ontario.

hab•i•tats places where plants and animals grow or live in nature.

har•bor sheltered area of water deep enough to provide ships a place to anchor.

harsh very uncomfortable conditions.

herds groups of animals.

his•to•ri•ans people who study history.

hos•tile angry and unfriendly.

im•mi•grants people who permanently settle in another country.

in•dus•try business that provides a certain product or service.

in•vad•ing entering an area and taking it over by force.

in•ves•ti•gate to examine carefully.

is•land area of land that is completely surrounded by water.

Jes•u•it a part of the Catholic church known as the Society of Jesus.

jour•nals written records of daily events.

kid•napped took someone without permission.

kil•o•me•ters units of length that are equal to .621 of a mile.

knight an honor given to a man who has done something very special for England.

live•stock animals raised on a farm to eat or sell for profit.

loin•cloths pieces of cloth worn around the hips.

long•hous•es long dwellings where many families live at the same time.

mar•i•ner a sailor who navigates a ship.

mead•ows large areas of grassland.

mer•chant a buyer or seller whose goal is to make money.

mil•i•tar•y people who are part of the armed forces who may be asked to go to war.

mi•li•tias groups of men having some military training who are called upon only in emergencies.

mis•sion•ar•y a person sent to spread a religious faith.

mis•sions churches.

moat a deep ditch filled with water built to protect the entrance to a town or castle.

mo•nop•o•ly complete control over a product or service.

mus•ket a heavy gun used by soldiers, especially during the 1500s and 1600s.

na•tives people who belong to a place because they were born there.

nav•i•ga•tors people who control the direction of a ship.

New•found•land a large island in east Canada.

New France French colonies in North America from 1534 to 1763.

New World a term once used to describe the continents of North America and South America.

no•bil•i•ty an honor given to a person who has done great things for his country.

Nor•way a European country located in western Scandinavia whose capital and largest city is Oslo.

North A•mer•i•ca one of seven continents in the world. Bounded by Alaska on the northwest, Greenland on the northeast, Florida on the southeast, and Mexico on the southwest.

North Pole the northernmost end of the Earth.

out•num•bered having more people on one side than the other.

pen•in•su•la a large piece of land surrounded by water on three sides.

pet•ro•glyphs carvings or drawings in rocks usually made by people who lived a long time ago.

plun•dered robbed.

pods groups of seals, whales, or dolphins.

ports cities or towns located next to water with areas for loading and unloading ships.

Por•tu•gal a country along the Atlantic Ocean on the southwestern edge of Europe whose capital is Lisbon.

pre•serve protect from injury or ruin so more can be learned.

pri•va•teer an owner of a private ship with weapons that are licensed to attack enemy ships.

pro•fits money made after all expenses have been paid.

pro•mot•ed moved up in rank.

Qué•bec the largest province in Canada.

raid•ing entering someone's property for the purpose of stealing.

re•sourc•es things found in nature that are valuable to humans.

re•u•nit•ed joined back together.

re•venge to get even with someone for unfair treatment.

ri•val enemy.

scalped cut the top of a human head that is usually covered with hair.

scur•vy a disease caused from lack of vitamin C that results in swollen and bleeding gums, bleeding under the skin, and extreme weakness.

small•pox a disease that can be easily spread to other people, causing fever, weakness, and puss filled bumps that usually leave scars.

sound a narrow passage of water between an island and the mainland.

Strait of Ma•gel•lan a narrow strip of sea discovered by Ferdinand Magellan that connects the Atlantic and Pacific oceans near the southern tip of South America.

stroke a brain injury caused when a blood vessel bursts or is blocked.

sur•ren•dered gave up.

trea•son a crime against your country's government.

trea•ties formal agreements.

ves•sel large boat.

Vi•king a sea pirate from Scandinavia.

vows promises.

voy•age journey that is usually made by water.

West In•dies a chain of islands in the Caribbean Sea that stretches from the southern tip of Florida to the northeastern corner of South America.

wes•tern hem•is•phere the half of the Earth that contains North America, Central America, and South America.

whirl•pools fast currents of water that move in a swirling motion.

wit•ness•es people who are called upon to tell the truth about what they heard or saw.

ANSWERS

ANSWERS TO COMPREHENSION QUESTIONS

LEIF ERIKSON

1. C
2. J
3. A
4. H
5. A
6. J
7. D
8. G

JOHN CABOT

1. A
2. J
3. C
4. J
5. C
6. F
7. D
8. H

GIOVANNI DA VERRAZANO

1. C
2. F
3. C
4. H
5. B
6. H
7. B
8. F

JACQUES CARTIER

1. A
2. J
3. A
4. J
5. B
6. J
7. A
8. G

SIR FRANCIS DRAKE

1. B
2. H
3. A
4. H
5. C
6. F
7. B

SAMUEL DE CHAMPLAIN

1. C
2. H
3. A
4. H
5. C
6. G
7. B
8. H

HENRY HUDSON

1. B
2. H
3. D
4. H
5. A
6. G
7. A
8. J

ROBERT LA SALLE

1. D
2. G
3. B
4. H
5. A
6. J
7. D
8. H

THE FUTURE OF NEW FRANCE

1. D
2. H
3. A
4. G
5. A
6. F
7. B
8. J

ANSWERS TO VOCABULARY QUIZZES

PART I		PART II		PART III		PART IV	
1.	H	1.	W	1.	J	1.	K
2.	C	2.	B	2.	A	2.	D
3.	W	3.	M	3.	CC	3.	DD
4.	E	4.	F	4.	FF	4.	E
5.	R	5.	Z	5.	T	5.	W
6.	A	6.	A	6.	W	6.	F
7.	P	7.	AA	7.	D	7.	M
8.	N	8.	O	8.	F	8.	V
9.	S	9.	J	9.	E	9.	GG
10.	L	10.	Q	10.	N	10.	A
11.	I	11.	L	11.	G	11.	HH
12.	K	12.	R	12.	Z	12.	EE
13.	O	13.	E	13.	C	13.	C
14.	U	14.	S	14.	S	14.	O
15.	B	15.	I	15.	H	15.	AA
16.	Q	16.	N	16.	GG	16.	H
17.	G	17.	U	17.	Q	17.	FF
18.	M	18.	X	18.	KK	18.	R
19.	Z	19.	T	19.	U	19.	BB
20.	V	20.	Y	20.	EE	20.	I
21.	D	21.	D	21.	B	21.	N
22.	T	22.	V	22.	BB	22.	U
23.	F	23.	H	23.	O	23.	P
24.	J	24.	BB	24.	JJ	24.	T
25.	Y	25.	C	25.	P	25.	L
26.	X	26.	K	26.	I	26.	Z
		27.	G	27.	X	27.	Q
		28.	P	28.	L	28.	G
				29.	LL	29.	X
				30.	DD	30.	J
				31.	K	31.	Y
				32.	HH	32.	B
				33.	M	33.	CC
				34.	V	34.	S
				35.	II		
				36.	R		
				37.	Y		
				38.	AA		

ANSWERS TO CONSIDER THE SOURCE

1. S
2. P
3. P
4. S
5. P
6. P
7. P

ANSWERS TO JACQUES CARTIER TIME TRAVEL

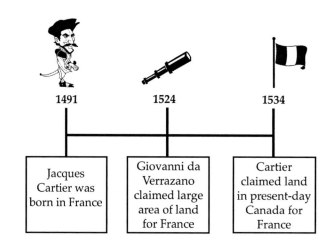

1491 — Jacques Cartier was born in France

1524 — Giovanni da Verrazano claimed large area of land for France

1534 — Cartier claimed land in present-day Canada for France

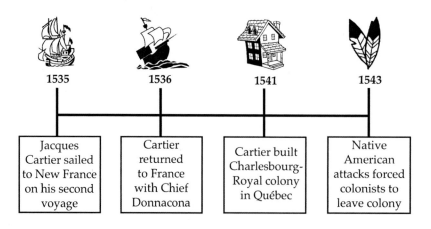

1535 — Jacques Cartier sailed to New France on his second voyage

1536 — Cartier returned to France with Chief Donnacona

1541 — Cartier built Charlesbourg-Royal colony in Québec

1543 — Native American attacks forced colonists to leave colony

ANSWERS TO CALIFORNIA MAP

CALIFORNIA MAP

ANSWERS TO CHAMPLAIN'S VOYAGES MAP

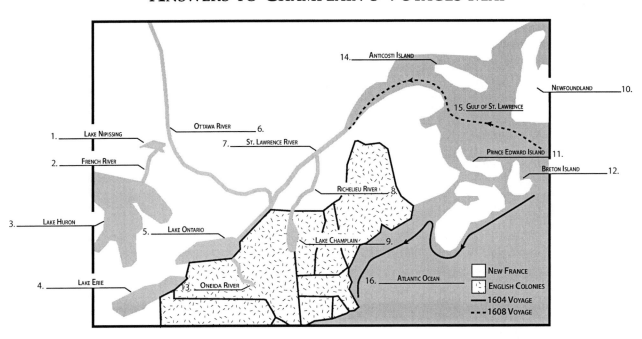

ANSWERS TO GOING THE DISTANCE

Voyage One	Voyage Two	Voyage Three	Voyage Four
6,240 Miles (+/- 300 miles) 10,046.4 Kilometers (+/- 480 kilometers)	6,060 Miles (+/- 300 miles) 9,756.6 Kilometers (+/- 480 kilometers)	4,420 Miles (+/- 200 miles) 7,116.2 Kilometers (+/- 320 kilometers)	5,040 Miles (+/- 300 miles) 8,114.4 Kilometers (+/- 480 kilometers)

GRADING CHART FOR EXPLORER K•W•L•H CHART

CRITERIA	POINTS POSSIBLE	POINTS EARNED
Answering 4 Questions Before Beginning Research	**20** (5 points each)	
Completing 5 Sections of K-W-L-H Chart (What I **Know**, What I **Want** to Know, What I **Learned**, **How** I Found Out)	**60** (12 points each)	
Answering 4 Questions After Finishing Research	**20** (5 points each)	
TOTAL	**100**	

BIBLIOGRAPHY

Bartleby: 'American Heritage Dictionary of the English Language: Fourth Edition' 2000
[Online] Available <http://www.bartleby.com> (August 1, 2008)

British Broadcasting Corporation: 'Historic Figures: Leif Erikson' 2008 [Online] Available
<http://www.bbc.co.uk/history/historic_figures/erikson_leif.shtml> (May 16, 2008)

Carson, Robert. The World's Great Explorers: Hernando de Soto. Chicago:
Children's Press, 1991.

Chadwick, Ian: 'The Life and Voyages of Henry Hudson, English Explorer and Navigator' 1992
[Online] Available <http://www.ianchadwick.com/hudson/hudson_overview.htm>
(January 10, 2009)

Enchanted Learning: 'René-Robert Cavelier, Sieur de La Salle: North American Explorer' 2000
[Online] Available
<http://www.enchantedlearning.com/explorers/page/l/lasalle.shtml> (May 4, 2008)

Engels, Andre: 'Jacques Cartier' 2005 [Online] Available
<http://www.win.tue.nl/cs/fm/engels/discovery/cartier.html> (January 3, 2009)

Engels, Andre: 'Louis Jolliet and Jacques Marquette' 2005 [Online] Available
<http://www.win.tue.nl/~engels/discovery/jolmar.html> (January 3, 2009)

Evisum, Inc: 'Robert Cavelier La Salle' 2000 [Online] Available
<http://www.famousamericans.net/robertcavelierlasalle/> (October 12, 2008)

Evisum, Inc: 'Samuel de Champlain' 2000 [Online] Available
<http://www.samueldechamplain.com/> (October 3, 2008)

Headley, Amy and Smith, Victoria. Do American History! Glendale, Arizona: Splash!
Publications, 2003.

Headley, Amy and Smith, Victoria. Do Arizona! Glendale, Arizona: Splash! Publications, 2006.

Headley, Amy and Smith, Victoria. Do California! Glendale, Arizona: Splash! Publications,
2005.

Headley, Amy and Smith, Victoria. Do Colorado! Glendale, Arizona: Splash! Publications,
2004.

Headley, Amy and Smith, Victoria. Do Nevada! Glendale, Arizona: Splash! Publications,
2007.

Headley, Amy and Smith, Victoria. Do New Mexico! Glendale, Arizona: Splash!
Publications, 2004.

Headley, Amy and Smith, Victoria. Do Texas! Glendale, Arizona: Splash!
Publications, 2006.

Heinrichs, Ann. <u>California: America the Beautiful</u>. New York: Children's Press, 1999.

Heinrichs, Ann. <u>Florida: America the Beautiful</u>. New York: Children's Press, 1998.

Heinrichs, Ann. <u>Texas: America the Beautiful</u>. New York: Children's Press, 1999.

Italian Historical Society of America: 'Giovanni da Verrazano' 2006 [Online] Available
    <http://www.italianhistorical.org/verrazzano.htm> (June 7, 2008)

Kent, Zachary. <u>Kansas: America the Beautiful</u>. Chicago: Children's Press, 1991

Landry, Peter: 'Samuel de Champlain' 1997 [Online] Available
    <http://www.blupete.com/Hist/BiosNS/1600-00/Champlain.htm> (April 10, 2008)

Lexico Publishing Group: 'Dictionary.com' 2004 [Online]
    Available <http:// dictionary.reference.com/> (September 1, 2008)

Museum of New France: 'The Explorers' 2000 [Online] Available
    <http://www.civilization.ca/vmnf/explor/explor_e.html> (May 7, 2008)

Nussbaum, Greg: 'Giovanni da Verrazano' 2008 [Online] Available
    <http://www.mrnussbaum.com/verrazano.htm> (February 3, 2009)

Nussbaum, Greg: 'Marquette and Joliet' 2008 [Online] Available
    <http://www.mrnussbaum.com/history/marquette.htm> (September 6, 2008)

Nussbaum, Greg: 'Samuel de Champlain' 2008 [Online] Available
    <http://www.mrnussbaum.com/champ2.htm> (February 3, 2009)

Nussbaum, Greg: 'Sir Francis Drake' 2008 [Online] Available
    <http://www.mrnussbaum.com/drake.htm> (February 3, 2009)

Sherwood Elementary School: 'Explorers of the Millennium' 1998 [Online] Available
    <http://library.thinkquest.org/4034/> (July 12, 2008)

Smithsonian Institute: 'Vinland Archaeology' 2008 [Online] Available
    <http://www.mnh.si.edu/vikings/voyage/subset/vinland/archeo.html>
    (November 3, 2008)

Steins, Richard. <u>Exploration and Settlement</u>. Texas: Steck-Vaughn, 2000.

Viking Network, The: 'Leif Ericsson' 2000 [Online] Available
    <http://www.viking.no/e/people/leif/e-leiv.htm> (October 7, 2008)

Weitemier, Kevin: 'Leif Erikson' 1997 [Online] Available
    <http://www.mnc.net/norway/LeifErikson.htm> (July 2, 2008)

Woods, Mario. <u>The World of Native Americans</u>. New York: Peter Bedrick Books, 1997.